PRODUCTOS
AGRÍCOLAS

THE CUBAN TABLE

THE
CUBAN TABLE

A Celebration of Food, Flavors, and History

ANA SOFÍA PELÁEZ

Photographs by
ELLEN SILVERMAN

ST. MARTIN'S PRESS
NEW YORK

www.stmartins.com

The Library of Congress Cataloging-in-Publication
Data is available upon request.

ISBN 978-1-250-03608-7 (hardcover)
ISBN 978-1-4668-5753-7 (e-book)

St. Martin's Press books may be purchased
for educational, business, or promotional use.
For information on bulk purchases, please
contact Macmillan Corporate and Premium
Sales Department at 1-800-221-7945, extension
5442, or write specialmarkets@macmillan.com

First Edition: November 2014

10 9 8 7 6 5 4 3 2 1

To my grandparents,
who had to leave it all
so I could have it all.
—A.S.P.

For my dear husband
Josh and son Luca, who
are my best dining partners.
And to all of our family and
friends who regularly gather
around our table to share
food and conversation.
—E.S.

CONTENTS

Foreword *ix*

Introduction *1*

View from the Bakery Window 11

Sitting Around the Lunch Counter 49

Soups and Stews 79

Beans, Rice, and Eggs 109

Chicken, Beef, and Pork 139

Fish and Seafood 181

Fruits and Vegetables 207

Sweets and Desserts 233

Cocktails 285

Foundation Recipes *297*

Cuban Pantry and Glossary *308*

Resources *313*

Acknowledgments *314*

Index *317*

Our Cuban Tables

FOREWORD BY MARICEL E. PRESILLA

Culinary historian, James Beard Award Winner, chef of Zafra and Cucharamama in Hoboken, NJ, and author of *Gran Cocina Latina: The Food of Latin America* (W. W. Norton, 2012)

A QUIET CLARITY SUFFUSES THE PAGES OF THIS BOOK, AND AN INEXORABLE TRUTH is told on every page: There is no single Cuban table, but many, straddling the Florida Straits, scattered across the globe, and built on memory fragments of what once was when we were all one people, living together on a crocodile-shaped Caribbean island.

Wherever Cubans have found homes outside the island, we have planted roots firmly in the here and now, for we are a pragmatic people. Nonetheless, we yearn for the Cuba of our imaginations—though no two Cuban exiles can agree on what this means. Nor can we find the essence of Cuban cooking by looking at only one side of the divide, but rather by putting together the pieces of the scattered puzzle we have become since the Castro revolution in 1959.

I left Cuba for the United States in 1970, but I lived my formative years in Santiago de Cuba in a family of artists, intellectuals, and gifted cooks. My Cuban table was bountiful and diverse, steeped in the culinary traditions of eastern Cuba. My maternal aunts were careful and sophisticated cooks, lovers of fine china and embroidered linen tablecloths. They were also fearless Amazons of the kitchen with an uncompromising farm-to-table sensibility and a reverence for fresh produce, home-raised poultry, and local fish and game caught by my uncle Oscar. My paternal grandmother, Pascuala Ferrer, was born on a cacao farm in Jauco, near Baracoa, Cuba's first Spanish city. She was a true country cook, gutsy and earthy, reveling in big soups like *ajiaco*, brimming with tubers and starchy vegetables and flavored with farm-smoked pork. As a bride in the small town of Baire, she had learned to cook traditional dishes from the central part of our region that were rarely seen elsewhere in Cuba—dishes that my father, Ismael Espinosa, craved and re-created in his Miami kitchen to his dying day.

I was lucky to experience these two worlds firsthand on the island, and they are the foundation of the Cuban table I have re-created in my U.S. home—neither wholly urban nor fully country, but a blend of the two. My cooking experience does not mirror that of Ana Sofía Peláez, who was born in the United States of Cuban parents, nor even that of members of my own family who have come here in more recent years. Each of us is shaped by our intimate connection to the cooking of our families and regions, but also by the moment of our departure, or that of our parents or grandparents.

I still think of the island as a cradle of comfort and lushness. I have thrown beans into the ground and seen them grow. I have stretched out my hand and picked delicious mango and papaya. In deep green forests and tall mountains rimming the horizon a dark blue, I have heard the gentle rustling of animals and the chirping of birds. I have ambled down Cuban roads, and seen people at ease with themselves, moving with a relaxed flow, their faces friendly, their manner open and hospitable. Though I could see the dignified Spaniard in their bearing, I could also see an African rhythm in their walk. I have heard the distinctive sounds of our hybrid culture: conga drumming during carnival, fresh red snapper sizzling in an iron pan, the *décimas* (country ballads) of the Cuban *guajiro* (peasant) strummed on a guitar as a pig roasted on a spit. I have sat at many Cuban tables, bitten into *casabe* (yuca bread), sipped a spoonful of *ajiaco,* and gotten a hint of the cooking of the Taínos (Arawak) who lived in these islands before the Spanish came.

In my memory, this is as close as I have gotten to paradise. Not even the hardships of war during the Cuban revolution could strip this world of its wonder, but decades of deprivation and repression after 1959 took their toll. We experienced the indignities of life on ration cards, enduring long lines to buy bare essentials and often felt hungry. Many who stayed saw their families divided, their pantries empty, the flavors of cherished family recipes compromised for lack of key ingredients, and the richness of their tables dulled by chronic shortages of staples from beef and fish to rice and beans, from cherished cooking fats like olive oil to raisins and olives. Even the memory of dishes that were once at the core of our identity faded into a twilight zone of sorts, waiting to be rescued as families separated and older cooks began to die.

The Cubans who left the island in waves beginning in 1959 and who came to the United States, first legally in chartered planes and later illegally by boat or flimsy raft, worked hard to reinvent themselves through food. They represented every region of the island, every race and occupation, from blue-collar workers to professionals, from fishermen and farmers to landed aristocracy. No longer segregated by class, color, or geography, we were brought together through the common experience of exile and, penniless, we learned from each other in ways that were not possible when we lived together on the island. Our Cubanness and our desire to build new lives went hand-in-hand, as we were banned for decades from returning to the island even for a visit.

Julián and Carmen Peláez del Casal, Ana Sofía's paternal grandparents, came from an affluent family in Havana. Julián was the brother of Amelia Peláez del Casal, an artist of great renown whom I had met as a child on a visit to her lovely Havana home with my father, who was also a painter. I remember her as a kind woman who reminded me of my Aunt Anita, and I was drawn to her abstract paintings of tropical fruits and flowers framed by elements of Cuban architecture. Ana Sofía's grandparents ultimately settled in Queens, New York, where they learned to cook Cuban food from a neighbor. (Servants had managed their Havana kitchen.) Her grandfather became an avid home cook who transmitted his understanding of Cuban food to his granddaughter. Growing up in Miami, Ana Sofía also ate at Cuban cafeterias, storefront restaurants, and bakeries, where decades of memory and longing and the mingling of disparate regional traditions, dominated by the western provinces, produced a generic Cuban cuisine.

When Ellen Silverman, whose *Cuban Kitchens* series garnered much critical acclaim, asked Ana Sofía to collaborate on a Cuban cookbook, they knew they would need to travel to Cuba together. Ana Sofía traveled to the island expecting to find the platonic ideal of the food her grandfather had taught her to make and the missing links that would allow her to paint a complete picture of the Cuban table. What she found were more questions than answers, and the sad certainty that much had been irretrievably lost. She also found solace in the knowledge that there was much that was alive and well in the Cuban communities in exile.

Traveling to Cuba, Ellen and Ana Sofía shunned official escorts and did their own fact-finding, seeking out home cooks, photographing, and eating at tourist restaurants and private *paladares* in Havana and beyond. What Ana Sofía chose to record for this book was the best of her experiences, the recipes of gifted cooks who struggled to put good food on the table, but who knew what was missing in their dishes. These recipes joined the dozens Ana Sofía collected from Cuban cooks living in the United States, thus bringing together two sides of the same construct with delicious results: dishes close to the Cuban heart that will entice you to cook, and well-chosen recipes that tell the poignant, decades-old saga of a divided people who are still connected through food.

I appreciate the lucidity of *The Cuban Table* and the clear eye and steady hand Ana Sofía has brought to a complicated subject. Ellen Silverman adds cohesion to this story of losses and gains with soulful pictures that capture the restraint and dignity of the Cuban kitchen and table and the enduring beauty of an island where the weathered and imperfect are not just what is left of the past, but the only present.

I am grateful to Ana Sofía for her choice of recipes: traditional dishes full of character and flavor that require little embellishment. All cuisines evolve and change, but when they are "endangered," as is the case with Cuban food, we must treasure the timeless classics, and preserve them for generations to come.

INTRODUCTION

GROWING UP IN MIAMI, CUBA WAS NEVER VERY FAR FROM OUR THOUGHTS, OUR conversations, or our kitchen table. Weekends spent with my grandparents, Julian and Carmen Peláez del Casal, started with a tour of the markets—looking for the best cuts for oxtail stew to make *rabo encendido*, piling up on plantains and the ubiquitous bags of white rice, then stopping by a roadside fruit stand to buy fresh green coconuts where a man would carve out an opening with a few short sweeps of his machete so we could drink *agua de coco* directly from the source.

Seeing my grandparents side by side at the counter of their sun-filled kitchen—working out their favorite Cuban recipes such as *potaje de frijoles negros* and *pollo asado*, or preparing the caramel for a rich *flan de leche*—they seemed very much at home. It was surprising then when I asked my grandfather who had taught him how to cook and he answered bittersweetly, "Exile."

I was raised on my grandparents' descriptions of elaborate meals in our great-grand-mother's home surrounded by extended family where there was never a quiet moment. I assumed they took part in the process, but in Cuba, active careers and help at home kept them away from the kitchen. It wasn't until emigrating to the United States in the 1960s that they learned to cook for themselves, a process they quickly fell in love with. Starting with the Creole dishes they missed the most, the repetition and ritual of these simple meals becoming an act of both preservation and reinvention.

Eventually finding my own way to Cuba in 2000, I spent time with my great-aunt Ninita, who still lived in our family's home in the Víbora section of Havana, surrounded by her mother's garden, her father's books, and the vibrant still lifes of her sister, the ven-erated painter Amelia Peláez del Casal. The now-silent rooms were filled with the personal belongings that family members left with her for safekeeping before leaving the island.

Not wanting to be a burden, I brought basics, such as beans, rice, and seasonings from Miami, and promptly handed everything over to Nena, a cook and caretaker with our family for more than four decades. Combined with the fruits, vegetables, farmer cheese, and chicken she'd sought out, Nena managed a week's worth of brilliant cooking, culminating in my aunt Ninita's *merengón*. Sitting around the same table I'd heard about so many times, every dish was somehow deeper, richer, and more flavorful.

A small inheritance led to my own rediscovery of Cuban cooking when my grand-parents' 1970s Sunbeam mixer found its way to my Brooklyn apartment not long after the trip. Looking at it, I could see them standing over the rotating bowl of egg whites, timing out just the right moment to add sugar, a pinch of salt, or a drop of vanilla to make endless trays of airy meringues. Setting out to retrace my grandparents' steps through the few recipes they had written down, one dish led to another, and my hunger for all things related to Cuban cooking grew. Launching my blog Hungry Sofia at the end of 2008, I cast a wide net to discover the rich smells, heady flavors, and baroque rituals of Latin American and Caribbean food, but I always came back to Cuban cuisine.

Living away from Miami's Cuban cultural hub, this was often done in translation. The Italian lard bread sold in Brooklyn bakeries became a near substitute for the *pan de manteca* used in Cuban sandwiches. The Colombian butcher knew *palomilla* meant top-round and which was the best cut for pork rind *chicharrones*. I learned to ask for *yautía* instead of *malanga* and *batatas* instead of *boniatos* at the Puerto Rican grocers along the Lower East Side. When all else failed, I could find fresh guavas and even sugar cane in Chinatown.

In 2011, I met Ellen Silverman, a New York City–based food photographer who'd recently been to Cuba and was interested in developing a Cuban cookbook. Taking stock of what was (or wasn't) in the Cuban kitchens she photographed, she met people who confessed that limited choices diminished the pleasure they once took in preparing meals. We began to collaborate on this book, which has become as much about the textures and colors of Cuba as the delicious food and memorable stories that they inspire.

More than just a list of ingredients or series of steps, Cuban cooks' tricks and touches hide in plain sight, staying within families or passed down in well-worn copies of old cookbooks. Starting in Miami, I interviewed family and friends who warned that they never wrote anything down and couldn't explain what they did. Talking my way into countless kitchens, I watched them work, quickly dropping a tablespoon under the *pimentón* they were tossing into a simmering pot or noting the number of diced cachucha peppers about to disappear into a sofrito.

I'd come for the food but the stories of political upheaval, exile, challenges, celebration, scarcity, and abundance were wonderful, too, as well as the images the stories inspired—orange groves rising out of the iron-rich red earth, and boulevards lined with avocado trees, smokehouses filled with freshly made sausages, and fishing villages celebrating a good catch, kids rushing down hills on royal palm leaves turned into sleds, and horse-drawn dairy carts loaded down with metal *cántaras* of fresh milk topped with cream so thick that just a little bit of salt sufficed to make butter.

I'd known my research would eventually lead me back to Havana, but the short flight from Miami hardly gave me enough time to prepare. It had been thirteen years since my last visit and with both my great-aunt Ninita and Nena gone, the direct connection I felt to the island had been severed.

With only a list of friends of friends and family of family, I tentatively started making the rounds with the letters, gifts, medicines, and supplies people entrusted me to deliver to their families on the island. At each short stop, which quickly became a long visit, people were excited to hear about my project and talk about the foods they loved. But it soon became clear we'd mostly be *talking* about food. While people were managing,

sharing when they were able and conserving what they could, food was anything but casual in Havana. Even a modest meal required planning, and I was careful not to over-strain anyone's resources.

In sharp contrast, family-run restaurants, or *paladares*, served flavorful meals with hard-to-come-by ingredients. In the early 1990s, when the withdrawal of subsidies from the former Soviet Union brought on a severe economic crisis known as the *Período Especial*, or Special Period, limited licenses allowed individuals to operate small restaurants out of residential kitchens. The word *paladares* comes from a Brazilian soap opera named *Vale Todo* and the reality was no less dramatic. There were stories of frequent raids, contraband lobsters being chucked out of windows, and arranged marriages to circumvent rules that prohibited hiring outside the family. With recent economic reforms, *paladares* can now hire employees, offer more seating, and expand their menus, but they still cannot access a wholesale market. Chefs and owners buy their food retail, which makes their prices out of reach for most Cubans and forces the chefs to cater almost exclusively to a tourist market.

While the worst days of the *Período Especial* were long gone, many of the foods temporarily suspended for the duration failed to reappear. Fish and beef, in all its forms, are still particularly hard to come by and many of the dishes that I'd considered staples of everyday Cuban cooking had all but disappeared. Stepping outside of Havana came as a relief. Now joined by Ellen, who would be taking photographs, we started west.

Passing through Artemisa, we stopped at a nondescript farmhouse known for their fried pork chunks, which were fork tender and beautifully caramelized. I never expected to swoon at the sight of a bubbling cauldron full of lard, but I came close. I'd heard my family describe the enormous tubs where they kept fried pork and homemade *butifarras* (sausages) confit-style but had never seen it. It was a technique so simple and perfect in itself that nothing could be taken away from it. Where so much of the trip had been defined by what was missing and no longer possible, it was a small sign of life, and Cuba started to open.

Slowly, the stories and anecdotes came alive—small batch factories turning out creamy guava paste in Ciego de Ávila, roadside stands selling *crema de leche* in Camagüey, sugar cane juice boiled down to make *raspadura* in an open field, and fresh fish pulled from the Bahía de Santiago. There were also discoveries, such as the spice and fire added to marinades in the eastern provinces and coconut *cucuruchos* cooked down with honey and almonds and wrapped in palm leaves in Baracoa.

Cuban food has always been about improvisation and adaptation—a rich confluence of indigenous, Spanish, African, Chinese, Caribbean, and even French cuisine that was constantly evolving. Fruits and vegetables native to the island— such as corn, yuca, boniato, *ajíes* or fresh peppers, guava, annón, guanábana, and papaya—were cultivated by the indigenous Siboney and Taíno populations and supplemented a diet of fish and small game hunting. The Spanish conquest brought livestock—including cattle, pigs, sheep, goats, and chickens—as well as oranges, limes, and sugar cane. Plantains and tubers such as *ñame* and *malanga* were brought from Africa along with various techniques for making these ingredients work together. A little later, immigrants fleeing the Haitian revolution in the late-eighteenth century brought French Creole recipes and coffee cultivation to the island. Chinese laborers introduced Cantonese cooking in the mid-nineteenth century while regional Spanish cuisine came with successive waves of immigration from northern Spain and the Canary Islands through the mid-twentieth century. At that point, the clocks stopped and all Cuban cooks became conservationists. Cuban life came to be seen through the prism of before and after 1959—the present realities an obstacle to remembering a picture-perfect past or imagining a more fulfilling future.

For many Cuban-Americans struggling to maintain their identity over several generations, food is a pure expression of the culture they left behind or inherited from their parents. Visiting Cuban-owned restaurants and markets, I was amazed to see how many had stayed within families, passed on to sons and daughters who may Tweet, Instagram, and rebrand but stay true to what their parents built. Friends whose children barely speak Spanish puff up with pride when they hear them ask for more roasted pork on *Nochebuena* or pass up the brownies for a large piece of *masa real* filled with guava. Their sense of relief is palpable as well as the hope that not all is lost.

I had expected Cuban food in the diaspora and food on the island to mirror each other, an extensive but fixed repertoire with a shared approach. What I found instead were fragments, each cook holding on to what they understood Cuban food to be and waiting for a time when they would once again be part of a greater whole. In that sense at least, we're more alike than I could have imagined.

Looking at Ellen Silverman's photographs, I don't see quiet halls or barren kitchens, but an aunt or uncle who stayed on the island, their brothers and sisters who left with their families to the United States, a neighbor who operates a *paladar* from her home, her husband who brings whatever fresh produce he can from the family's farm outside of Havana, or their nephew who trained in Cuba but has gone on to become an executive chef in New York or Miami. I see all of us who know we've tasted something wonderful, even as we walk away.

Far beyond the last fifty years of Cold War brinksmanship, familial separation, and mass migration Cuban food has not only survived in surprising ways, but taken root in new cities, becoming a treasured part of the international food landscape. At the Cuban table these disparate elements and ingredients come together—for those who stayed, for those who left, and for those who've only imagined visiting but gratefully find themselves a little closer through the smells and tastes of Cuban cuisine.

—*Ana Sofía Peláez*

CUBANS ARE PASSIONATE ABOUT THEIR FOOD AND GRACIOUS ABOUT SHARING IT. Spending long hours around the table eating and talking with family and friends is important to them. This is the Cuba that I wanted to share in this book.

I arrived in Havana for the first time on the evening of December 10, 2010. As I drove from the airport into the city, I immediately noticed how dark it was. There were few lit streetlights or lights on in the windows of houses or apartments.

During my one-week stay, I woke before dawn each day and watched the city's tropical colors unfold as the sun rose. Daylight revealed once beautiful but now decrepit buildings that I desired to explore. The exteriors were just a tease as to what the buildings might show me once I entered. I was mesmerized by the range of colors, textures, and sounds as Havana came alive each morning with its unique rhythm and energy palpable on the streets.

I am drawn to the objects that people choose to surround themselves with. What we keep and what we discard tells the story of who we are and what is important to us. On this first trip, I was welcomed into Cuban homes where time seemed to have stopped. Years of subsistence living and a dearth of the simplest supplies and equipment have forced Cubans to adapt and improvise. In particular, my eye was drawn to the natural, organic arrangements in Cuban kitchens: A spoon casually left on the counter, an empty Coca-Cola can used as a toothbrush holder, or a bunch of green bananas waiting to be fried hung on a nail against a pink wall, all became the subjects of my photographs.

In addition to Cuban kitchens, I sought out the markets where locals shop, as I do wherever I travel. I found artfully arranged fruits and vegetables sold by energetic vendors who called out to potential customers with a smile, a wink, and a flirtatious word.

Some people winked at me as well as I walked by, while others stopped to engage me in conversation, asked about my camera, and eagerly invited me into their homes. The Cubans I met were generous, warm, curious, and eager to talk. I immediately felt at ease with them. That first trip ignited my desire to learn more about Cuba, Cubans, their culture, and their food.

As soon as I returned to New York, I was determined to find a reason to go back, to photograph and build on the understanding and friendships that started during the first trip. The memories of Cuban kitchens and the people who cooked in them stayed with me. Six months later, I returned to continue photographing kitchens in preparation for a one-woman show in New York.

After my show, I wanted to take the subject even further in the form of a cookbook and was inspired by *The Book of Jewish Food: An Odyssey from Samarkand and Vilna to the Present Day*, by Claudia Roden. In all of her books, but especially *The Book of Jewish Food*, Claudia Roden writes evocatively of each dish's origins, its complicated history, and the changes it has undergone over time, distance, and the availability of ingredients. Every time I look for a recipe in that book I become absorbed in those stories. Anecdotes, explanations of ingredients, and culinary traditions add layers of interest beyond the recipes

Before going to Cuba I had been warned that I would be disappointed by the flavor and savor of the food. Quite the contrary! My fellow Cuban photographer and friend Carlos Otero Blanco loves food and knows where many of the best, often hidden, places to eat are to be found on the island. Together we shared some amazing meals, many at *paladares*—small, private, family-run restaurants found in people's homes or on farms. At times we serendipitously chose places that looked inviting and were rewarded with wonderful food and gracious hosts. Armando, a farmer in Viñales, cooked one of our most memorable meals—he had harvested all of the ingredients from his land that morning—an omelet from fresh-laid eggs, boiled yucca, boniato, the thinnest hand-cut yucca chips, and *congri*—Cuban rice and beans—all cooked over a wood fire. We finished with freshly brewed coffee made with beans from his own trees.

I began to search for an enthusiastic and knowledgeable Cuban food writer, who could collaborate with me. I was introduced to Cuban-American food writer, Ana Sofía Peláez. Ana excitedly embraced the project, became my partner, and tirelessly collected recipes and stories from her Cuban family, friends, and friends of friends both here and in Cuba. Ana's meticulously researched recipes and stories paint a vivid picture of the depth and breadth of Cuban cuisine and evocatively compliment the story told by my photographs.

Ana and I sought to document how some traditional recipes have remained constant, while others have changed and evolved as circumstances and ingredients required and allowed. Family recipes, traditions, and stories are preserved by being passed from generation to generation in the kitchen preparing meals, as well as around the dining table. *The Cuban Table* tells this story.

—*Ellen Silverman*

VIEW FROM THE
BAKERY WINDOW

Like beehives scattered across the Miami landscape, Cuban bakeries and cafés operate out of *ventanitas*—street-front windows typically manned by two or three women who produce a steady stream of pitch-perfect *cafecitos* and *cortados* while calmly taking multiple orders, making change, and giving advice. Chatty crowds gather for the guava-filled pastries, crisp empanadas, and freshly fried *croquetas* served in brightly colored baskets lined in wax paper in mini public squares where everything is discussed but the only thing ever settled is the bill. On the counter, under plastic cake stands, buttery *panques de Jamaica*, dome-topped pound cakes stamped with a distinctive rooster logo, guard the windows alongside industrial-size juicers that, like the conversation, are constantly whirring. Before moving on, customers pick up a *colada*—multiple shots of pulled espresso poured into large styrofoam containers and taken away with a short stack of plastic demitasse cups. Spreading through-out the city, they'll find their way to friends and strangers, offices and warehouses, precincts and firehouses, hair salons and cigar shops, waiting rooms and departure gates—pouring out the coffee that keeps the city buzzing.

SURTIDO DE PASTELITOS | *assorted pastries* . . . 15

PASTELITOS DE QUESO . . . 15

PASTELITOS DE GUAYABA . . . 16

PASTELITOS DE QUESO Y GUAYABA . . . 19

MASA REAL CON GUAYABA | *guava layered cake* . . . 22

PANQUECITOS | *miniature poundcakes* . . . 23

FRESH FRUIT MARMALADES: GUAYABA, MANGO,
FRUTA BOMBA . . . 27

EMPANADITAS DE CHORIZO | *chorizo empanadas* . . . 32

CHIVIRICOS . . . 34

CROQUETAS DE JAMÓN | *ham croquettes* . . . 36

CROQUETAS DE MEDIA NOCHE | *midnight croquettes* . . . 38

PAPAS RELLENAS | *stuffed potatoes* . . . 42

CAFÉ CUBANO: ESPRESSO, CORTADO, CAFÉ CON LECHE . . . 45

EL PECADO | *layered coffee* . . . 47

SURTIDO DE PASTELITOS

At first glance these turnovers are pretty similar, yet lines form while customers waver between glazed-over puff pastry filled with molten guava or sugar-crusted *pastelitos de queso* stuffed with sweetened cream cheese. For those who just can't make up their minds, they can order a *pastelito de guayaba y queso* and have both at once. Made at home, you don't have to decide at all.

PASTELITOS DE QUESO

MAKES 18 PASTRIES

2 sheets frozen puff pastry dough, thawed (from one 17¼-ounce package)

1 large whole egg, lightly beaten with 1 tablespoon of water

FOR THE FILLING

9 ounces cream cheese, at room temperature

1 tablespoon sugar, plus more for sprinkling

1 teaspoon lemon juice

¼ teaspoon orange blossom water

Preheat the oven to 400°F. Line a 13 x 18 x 1-inch baking sheet with parchment paper or a nonstick liner.

To prepare the filling, beat together the cream cheese, sugar, lemon juice, and orange blossom water in a medium mixing bowl until the filling is light and fluffy.

Roll out the first sheet of pastry dough on a lightly floured surface to a 12-inch square, ⅛ inch thick. Using a small knife or pastry wheel, cut the dough to measure out 9 squares, 4 by 4 inches each. Add 1 tablespoon of cream cheese filling, off center, to each square. Brush the egg wash around the filling. Fold the pastry square over itself to form a triangle. Brush the tip of the triangle with the egg wash then fold the point of the triangle back over the other side to form a tight cylinder. Lightly brush the top of the pastry with the egg wash and sprinkle generously with sugar. Transfer the filled pastries to the prepared baking sheet and refrigerate them until firm, 20 to 30 minutes. Repeat with the remaining pastry dough.

Place the pastries in the preheated oven and bake until lightly golden, 20 to 25 minutes. Rotate the baking sheet halfway through the baking time to ensure that the pastries bake evenly.

PASTELITOS DE GUAYABA

MAKES 16 PASTRIES

2 sheets frozen puff pastry dough, thawed
(from one 17¼-ounce package)
1 large whole egg, lightly beaten with
1 tablespoon of water

FOR THE FILLING

8 ounces *Guava Preserves* (page 27) or
guava paste (see note, page 19)

FOR THE GLAZE

¼ cup sugar
¼ cup water

Preheat the oven to 400°F. Line a 13 x 18 x 1-inch baking sheet with parchment paper or a nonstick liner.

Roll out the first sheet of pastry on a lightly floured work surface to a 12-inch square ⅛ inch thick. Dock the dough by using a fork to make small incisions so that it rises evenly. Lightly score the dough to measure out 16 squares, 3 x 3 inches each. Top each square with 1 tablespoon of guava, allowing a 1-inch border. Lightly brush the egg wash around the borders of each square.

Roll out the remaining pastry sheet to an identical 12-inch square and cover the filled sheet. Press down around the filling to seal. Brush the tops with the remaining egg wash. Using a small knife or pastry wheel, cut the dough to measure out 16 squares, 3 x 3 inches each. It is not necessary to pull the squares apart before baking them. Transfer the filled pastries to the prepared baking sheet and refrigerate them until firm, 20 to 30 minutes.

While the pastries chill, prepare the glaze by combining the sugar and water in a small saucepan. Simmer over medium heat until the sugar is dissolved, about 5 minutes. Remove from the heat and allow to cool.

Place the pastries in the preheated oven and bake until lightly golden, 20 to 25 minutes. Rotate the baking sheet halfway through the baking time to ensure that the pastries bake evenly.

Remove the pastries from the oven and brush with the simple syrup. Allow the pastries to rest for 10 minutes on the baking sheet then slice the pastries and transfer them to a cooling rack.

PASTELITOS DE QUESO Y GUAYABA

MAKES 18 PASTRIES

2 sheets frozen puff pastry dough, thawed
(from one 17¼-ounce package)

1 large whole egg, lightly beaten with
1 tablespoon of water

FOR THE FILLING

9 ounces cream cheese, at room
temperature

1 tablespoon sugar

1 teaspoon lemon juice

¼ teaspoon orange blossom water

9 ounces Guava Preserves (page 27) or
guava paste (see note, below)

FOR THE GLAZE

¼ cup sugar

¼ cup water

Preheat the oven to 400°F. Line a 13 x 18 x 1-inch baking sheet with parchment paper or nonstick liner.

To prepare the filling, beat together the cream cheese, sugar, lemon juice, and orange blossom water until light and fluffy.

Roll out the first sheet of pastry on a lightly floured surface to a 12-inch square, ⅛ inch thick. Using a small knife or pastry wheel, cut the dough to measure out 9 squares, 4 by 4 inches each. Add 1 tablespoon of guava topped with 1 tablespoon of cream cheese filling, off center, to each square. Brush the egg wash around the filling. Fold the pastry square over itself to form a triangle and seal. Lightly brush the top of each triangle with egg wash. Transfer the filled pastries to the prepared baking sheet and refrigerate them until firm, 20 to 30 minutes. Repeat with the remaining pastry dough.

While the pastries chill, prepare the glaze by combining the sugar and water in a small saucepan. Simmer over medium heat until the sugar is dissolved, about 5 minutes. Remove from the heat and allow to cool.

Place the pastries in the preheated oven and bake until lightly golden, 20 to 25 minutes. Rotate the baking sheet halfway through the baking time to ensure that the pastries bake evenly.

NOTE

If using guava paste, cut the guava into chunks and process in a blender or food processor with 1 teaspoon of freshly squeezed orange or lime juice until smooth. Use the guava filling as directed. The pastries can also be filled with a variety of *Fresh Fruit Marmalades* (page 27) or *Dulce de Coco* (page 262).

Guava Layered Cake

MASA REAL CON GUAYABA

MAKES 12 TO 16 PIECES

Alicia Navia Jiménez's father owned La Estrella *chocolate factory in Havana. Not surprisingly, she had many dessert recipes, including this often requested* Masa Real. *The name translates to "royal crust," which sums up its supremacy in Cuban bakeries. Neither cake, scone, nor cookie, but all of those things at once, it's as welcome in the morning as in late afternoon for a snack or* merienda. *Most commonly filled with guava or* Dulce de Coco *(page 262), it also lends itself to savory fillings (see note, page 262) like* Fricasé de Pollo *(page 150).*

1 tablespoon coconut oil or unsalted butter, melted

2½ cups unbleached all-purpose flour

1 cup sugar

2 teaspoons baking powder

1 teaspoon kosher salt

8 tablespoons (1 stick) unsalted butter, cubed and held cold until needed

4 tablespoons best-quality leaf lard, cubed and held cold until needed

2 large whole eggs, well-beaten

2 tablespoons sweet sherry or wine

12 ounces guava paste, cut into ¼-inch-thick slices

1 large whole egg, lightly beaten with 1 tablespoon of water

Preheat the oven to 425°F. Lightly oil a 9-inch square baking pan with coconut oil or butter and set aside.

Sift together the dry ingredients in a large mixing bowl. Using a pastry blender or two knives, cut the butter and lard into the flour mixture until it flakes into pea-sized pieces. Add the eggs and sherry and stir until it forms a smooth dough. Do not overwork the dough.

Pour the dough onto a lightly floured board and divide it in half. Roll out each half to a 9-inch square, ½ inch thick.

Transfer the first piece of dough to the prepared baking pan. Smooth the surface with an offset spatula to form an even layer. Cover the dough with the sliced guava. Roll out the remaining dough and drape over the guava layer, tucking in the sides to seal the top and bottom layers. Brush the top with egg wash.

Place the pastry in the preheated oven and bake at 425°F for 10 minutes. Reduce the heat to 350°F and continue to bake 35 to 40 minutes longer, until golden brown. Remove from the oven and cool on a rack for 10 minutes. Slice and serve from the pan or unmold.

NOTE

The prepared dough can be tightly wrapped in plastic and frozen for up to 3 months. If using a savory filling, the amount of sugar called for in the recipe should be halved.

Miniature Poundcakes

PANQUECITOS

MAKES 12 *PANQUECITOS*

Plain as madeleines but denser and richer, panques *go well enough with tea but are built to stand up to a steaming cup of* café con leche. *The batter should be chilled well before baking to achieve a smooth buttery dome.*

2 cups unbleached all-purpose flour

½ teaspoon baking powder

½ teaspoon kosher salt

16 tablespoons (2 sticks) unsalted butter, melted and cooled to room temperature, plus 2 tablespoons for greasing the mold

1⅓ cups sugar

4 large whole eggs, at room temperature

1 teaspoon pure vanilla extract (optional)

SPECIAL EQUIPMENT:

12-cup standard muffin pan

Sift together the flour, baking powder, and salt in a medium mixing bowl and set aside.

In a stand mixer fitted with the whisk attachment, beat the eggs on medium speed for one minute until frothy. Gradually add the sugar and continue to beat until the yolks are pale yellow and form a ribbon, 5 additional minutes. Stir in the vanilla extract if using. Gently fold in the flour mixture in batches, alternating with the butter and ending with the flour, until it is just incorporated. Do not overmix the batter. Place a piece of plastic wrap on the surface of the batter so that it does not form a skin and refrigerate until chilled, at least 2 hours or overnight.

Preheat the oven to 375°F. Melt 2 tablespoons of butter in a small saucepan and generously butter the muffin pan.

Place about ¼ cup of the batter in each muffin cup. The batter will spread as it bakes so do not overfill. Set in the preheated oven and bake until a tester comes out clean, 20 to 25 minutes. Remove from the oven and allow to rest 10 minutes in the pan then transfer the *panques* to a cooling rack. Unmold the *panques* and set upright on the cooling rack.

NOTE

The batter can be poured directly into the prepared mold and chilled altogether before baking. The *panquecitos* can be kept in an airtight container up to 3 days or frozen up to 1 month.

ROGER CRUZ DOES NOT REMEMBER THE exact day his grandmother pulled the page from the almanac that had the recipe for the *panquecitos* her family would faithfully make for more than a hundred years. But he does know that on January 6, 1912, José María and Pilar Cruz started selling the buttery cakes to the quarrymen and cattle drivers passing through their small town of Jamaica on their way to Havana. When Roger was taught the recipe by his father as a little boy, they were still made with fresh milk from the family's ranch, Creole eggs, and Cuban sugar. Newly arrived in the United States, he continued to sell them through the 1960s and '70s. Eventually he opened the current Panque de Jamaica factory in 1982, which he still runs with his youngest son, supplying both small Cuban bakeries and large-chain Florida supermarkets. Occasionally he mixes a batch himself, which he admits with a modest shrug, come out just a little bit prettier. Though the recipe is a closely guarded family secret, he did offer that the *panques* should taste only like butter—the best-quality possible—to make the most of the cakes' short ingredient list, which hasn't changed since that forgotten day so long ago.

FRESH FRUIT MARMALADES

Making marmalade is a simple way of preserving tropical fruit that is too lovely to pass up but too sweet to last. I learned to make these small-batch fruit marmalades with Magaly Acosta, who I stayed with in Havana. It's not uncommon when visiting Cuba to make arrangements to stay in a *casa particular*—a private home with rooms to rent. As a Cuban-American, this is something like meeting long-lost family whom you only have one thing in common with but quickly get to know. At Magaly's, this was played out over the breakfast table where an additional item would appear each day. By the end of the first week, I'd joined her in the kitchen where we'd catch up on our day while taking turns stirring pots of simmering guava or mango marmalade.

Guava Marmalade

MERMELADA DE GUAYABA

MAKES 3 CUPS

2 pounds ripe guavas, dark spots removed and ends trimmed

1½ to 2 cups turbinado sugar

1 to 2 teaspoons freshly squeezed lime juice

Slice the guavas in half and place in a 5- to 6-quart heavy pot with water to cover. Bring to a boil over medium heat. Simmer uncovered until the guavas are tender, about 20 minutes.

Remove the guavas with a slotted spoon and transfer to the jar of a blender or food processor. Pour in ½ cup of the cooking water and process on high speed until smooth.

Pass the guava purée (about 4 cups) through a fine-mesh sieve and return to the pot. Discard the solids. Stir in the sugar to taste and bring the guava to a steady simmer over medium-low heat. The purée will bubble and pop so cover the pot with a mesh screen or lid to avoid splatter. Remove the thick foam that forms on the surface with a spoon or skimmer. Continue to cook until the mixture is thick but still pourable, 15 to 20 minutes.

Stir in the lime juice to taste. Set aside to cool at least 1 hour in the refrigerator or 2 hours at room temperature. Pour into sterilized glass jars and seal.

Variation: GUAVA PRESERVES

Prepare the guavas as directed in the marmalade recipe. After adding the lime juice, allow the guava mixture to cook an additional 10 minutes, stirring constantly, until the color deepens and it pulls away from the pot in one smooth piece. To test, place a metal spoon in the freezer for at least 10 minutes, then dip the spoon into the guava. The guava is ready when it clumps on the cold spoon. Set aside to cool at least 1 hour in the refrigerator or 2 hours at room temperature. Pour into sterilized glass jars and seal.

Mango Marmalade

MERMELADA DE MANGO

MAKES 3 CUPS

Far from the weekend-long sessions I'd associated with jelly and jam making, this marmalade can be done in small batches. Magaly turned out delicious mango marmalade with only the fruit clinging to the seeds that were easily removed after a fast simmer.

4 ripe medium mangos, peeled and quartered

1½ to 2 cups superfine sugar
Zest and juice of 1 whole lime

Place the mangos, including the pits, in a 5- to 6-quart heavy pot with water to cover. Bring to a boil over medium heat. Simmer uncovered until the mango is tender, 15 to 20 minutes. Drain immediately. When cool enough to handle, scrape the pits to remove the fruit. Discard the seeds. Place the mango in the jar of a blender or food processor and process on high speed until smooth.

Pass the mango purée (about 4 cups) through a fine-mesh sieve and return to the pot, stirring frequently. Stir in the sugar to taste and bring to a steady simmer over medium-low heat. The mango purée will bubble and pop so cover the pot with a mesh screen or lid to avoid splatter. Remove the thick foam that forms on the top with a spoon or skimmer. Continue to cook until the mixture is thick but still pourable, 15 to 20 minutes. Stir in the lime zest and juice to taste. Set aside to cool at least 1 hour in the refrigerator or 2 hours at room temperature. Pour into sterilized glass jars and seal.

Variation: MANGO PRESERVES

For a more preserve-like texture, peel and pit the mango. Combine the cubed mango and sugar in the pot and mash together to form a textured purée. Bring to a steady simmer over medium-low heat, stirring constantly until the mango develops a bright sheen and you can see the bottom of the pot as you stir. To test, place a metal spoon in the freezer for at least 10 minutes, then dip the spoon into the mango. The mango is ready when it clumps on the cold spoon. Stir in the lime juice to taste. Set aside to cool at least 1 hour in the refrigerator or 2 hours at room temperature. Pour into sterilized glass jars and seal.

Papaya Marmalade

MERMELADA DE FRUTA BOMBA

MAKES 2 CUPS

**2 pounds ripe papaya, peeled, seeded, and
cut into 2-inch chunks**

1 tablespoon freshly squeezed lime juice

1 whole cinnamon stick

¾ to 1 cup sugar

Place the papaya chunks and lime juice in the jar of a blender or food processor. Pulse on high speed until smooth. Pass the papaya purée (about 3 cups) through a fine-mesh sieve and pour into a 5- to 6-quart heavy pot. Add the cinnamon stick and stir in the sugar to taste. Bring the papaya to a steady simmer over medium-low heat. The purée will bubble and pop so cover the pot with a mesh screen or lid to avoid splatter. Remove the thick foam that forms on the surface with a spoon or skimmer. Continue to cook until the mixture is thick but still pourable, 25 to 30 minutes. Set aside to cool at least 1 hour in the refrigerator or 2 hours at room temperature. Pour into sterilized glass jars and seal.

NOTE

Traditional recipes call for equal parts fruit purée and sugar, which can be overpowering, so I found myself taking a little sugar away with each batch depending on the ripeness of the fruit. In the end, I decided to reverse the process, adding only enough sugar to bring out the fruits' natural sweetness and reach the desired consistency.

Chorizo Empanadas

EMPANADITAS DE CHORIZO

MAKES 24 *EMPANADITAS*

Perfectly portable, empanaditas *are a popular street food but worth making at home where the prepared discs can be kept frozen then filled with many kinds of leftovers, such as* Ropa Vieja *(page 162) or* Camarones Enchilados *(page 189). In this variation, semi-cured Spanish chorizo is simmered in a tomato-based* sofrito *then tucked into the lard pastry and deep-fried.*

4 cups unbleached all-purpose flour

1 tablespoon sugar

2 teaspoons kosher salt

8 ounces best-quality leaf lard, cubed and held cold until needed

½ cup dry white wine

6 to 8 tablespoons of ice water as needed

3 cups Chorizo Filling (page 33)

2 cups canola or peanut oil for deep-frying or minimum amount required to fill deep fryer per the manufacturer's instructions

Sift together the dry ingredients in a large mixing bowl. Using a pastry blender or two knives, cut the lard into the flour mixture until it flakes into pea-sized pieces. Stir in the wine. Slowly add the ice water as needed to form a smooth dough that holds together. Do not overwork the dough. Shape the dough into 2 round discs, 1 inch thick, and double wrap in plastic. Chill the dough until firm, at least 1 hour or overnight.

Divide each disc in half and keep the remaining dough wrapped and chilled until ready to use. On a lightly floured surface, roll out the dough to a 9 x 12-inch rectangle, ⅛ inch thick. Cut out 6 pastry rounds using a 4-inch round cutter or glass. Set aside the remaining scraps of dough to make Chiviricos (page 34). Layer the prepared discs with parchment paper between each disc and keep chilled until ready to use. Repeat with the remaining dough.

To fill the *empanaditas,* hold each disc in the palm of your hand. Add one heaping tablespoon of the desired filling to the center of each round and fold over on itself to form a half moon while tucking the filling inside. Lightly brush the borders with water and seal the *empanaditas* by pressing down the edges with the tines of a fork.

Heat the oil over medium heat in a deep fryer or a 3- to 4-quart heavy pot until a deep-fat thermometer registers 375°F.

Fry the *empanaditas* in batches, turning them over once with a slotted spoon, until they are golden brown on both sides, 3 to 4 minutes.

Transfer the *empanaditas* to a plate lined with paper towels. Return the oil to 375°F in between batches and repeat with the remaining *empanaditas.*

CHORIZO FILLING

MAKES 3 CUPS

2 tablespoons extra-virgin olive oil

¾ pound semi-cured Spanish chorizo, casings removed and diced

1 small yellow onion, diced

1 small green bell pepper, diced

4 large whole garlic cloves, minced

1 teaspoon kosher salt

¼ teaspoon freshly ground black pepper

1 cup whole peeled tomatoes, fresh or canned, with their juice

¼ cup dry white wine

1 dried bay leaf

½ pound russet potatoes, peeled and cubed into ½-inch pieces

2 tablespoons fresh flat-leaf parsley, leaves and tender stems, finely chopped

Heat the oil in a heavy 10-inch skillet over medium heat. Add the chorizo and cook until it is lightly browned and has rendered its fat, 2 to 3 minutes. Add the onion, green pepper, garlic, salt, and black pepper and sauté until the onion is soft and translucent, about 5 minutes. Stir in the tomatoes, wine, and bay leaf and bring to a simmer for an additional 5 minutes. Add the potatoes and cook until the vegetables are tender and most of the liquid has evaporated, 15 to 20 minutes. Stir in the fresh parsley and adjust the seasonings to taste.

NOTE

After rolling and cutting the dough, the prepared discs can be layered with wax or parchment paper, tightly wrapped in plastic, and stored frozen for up to 3 months. Alternately, the empanadas can be filled in advance and frozen for later use for up to 1 month. If frozen, the filled empanadas should be thawed in the refrigerator or at room temperature for 20 minutes before frying to avoid oil splatter.

CHIVIRICOS

MAKES 24 TO 32 PIECES

I'd largely forgotten about chiviricos, *which are sold by street vendors in wax paper or prepackaged in Latin American markets, until Cristina Sabater described seeing enormous glass jars full of them on her great-aunt Zoila's counter. Made from the remaining scraps of empanada dough, they not only signal the sweet and savory* empanaditas *waiting to be eaten, but are delightful on their own.*

1 recipe Empanadita dough (page 32) or remaining scraps

2 cups canola or peanut oil

¼ cup sugar

1 tablespoon ground cinnamon

Roll out the reserved dough on a lightly floured surface to ⅛ inch thick. Cut the dough into decorative strips or desired shapes.

Heat the oil in a 10-inch skillet or deep fryer over medium heat to 375°F.

Fry the strips of dough in batches until crisp. Remove the strips with a slotted spoon and transfer to a plate lined with paper towels. Return the oil to 375°F in between batches and repeat with the remaining strips of dough.

Combine the sugar and cinnamon in a small bowl. Sprinkle the *chiviricos* with the cinnamon-sugar mixture while they are still warm.

Once cool, *chiviricos* can be stored at room temperature in a sealed glass jar for up to one week.

· Ham Croquettes

CROQUETAS DE JAMÓN

MAKES 32 *CROQUETAS*

Croquetas de Jamón, *made with a lightly seasoned béchamel sauce, are an undisputed favorite, whether delivered freshly fried with a packet of saltine crackers and a few sliced pickles at a* ventanita *or shaped into miniature torpedoes and set out on teeming trays at parties. Instead of making the traditional roux, Cuban cooks combine the milk and flour in a blender before adding it to the melted butter to produce a smoother sauce.*

¾ pound cooking ham, trimmed and cubed

1½ cups whole milk

1 cup plus 4 tablespoons unbleached all-purpose flour, divided

2 tablespoons unsalted butter, cubed

½ medium white onion, diced

1 teaspoon kosher salt

¼ teaspoon freshly ground white pepper

⅛ teaspoon freshly ground nutmeg

1 pinch cayenne pepper (optional)

2 tablespoons fresh flat-leaf parsley, leaves and tender stems, finely chopped

4 extra-large whole eggs, well-beaten

2 cups bread crumbs, finely ground, divided

2 cups canola oil

Pulse the ham in a food processor until minced. Separately, combine the milk and 4 tablespoons of flour in the jar of a blender and pulse until well combined.

Melt the butter in a heavy 4-quart saucepan over medium heat. Add the onion and sauté until soft, about 5 minutes. Slowly pour in the milk mixture and stir until the sauce has thickened and the whisk leaves trace marks on the surface, 5 more minutes. Stir in the salt, white pepper, nutmeg, and cayenne pepper, if using. Remove the saucepan from the heat and blend in the ham mixture and parsley. Adjust the seasonings to taste and allow the mixture to cool to room temperature.

Pour the béchamel mixture into a shallow bowl. Cover with plastic wrap and refrigerate until the mixture is set, at least one hour or overnight.

Preheat the oven to 200°F. Line a 13 x 18 x 1-inch baking sheet with parchment paper or a nonstick liner.

Place the beaten eggs, remaining flour, and 1 cup of bread crumbs in separate mixing bowls. Lightly oil your hands and spoon the béchamel mixture into walnut-size pieces then roll into the desired shape. Dip the *croqueta* in the egg then roll in the flour, shaking off the excess by passing it between your hands 2 to 3 times. Dip the *croqueta* in the egg a second time then roll it in the bread crumbs. The *croqueta* should be completely coated in bread crumbs so they do not leak when fried. Repeat with the remaining filling and replenish the bread crumbs as needed. Transfer the breaded *croquetas* to the lined tray and refrigerate until ready to use.

Heat 2 inches of oil over medium heat in a deep 10-inch skillet or heavy pot until a deep-fat thermometer registers 365°F.

Carefully add the *croquetas* in batches, turning occasionally, until brown on all sides, about 2 minutes. Remove with a slotted spoon and transfer to a plate lined with paper towels then place in a baking pan in the preheated oven to keep warm while you fry the remaining *croquetas*. Return the oil to 365°F in between batches. Serve immediately.

Variation: CROQUETAS DE POLLO | CHICKEN CROQUETTES

Omit the ham and replace with ¾ pound of shredded cooked chicken. Proceed with the recipe as directed.

Variation: CROQUETAS DE ESPINACA | SPINACH CROQUETTES

Omit the ham and replace with 1 pound of roughly chopped baby spinach or swiss chard. Rinse the spinach and add to the onions and sauté over medium-high heat until most of the liquid is evaporated, 3 to 5 minutes. Add the milk mixture and seasonings. Off heat, stir in 2 ounces of finely shredded Gruyère cheese. Proceed with the recipe as directed.

NOTE

The *croquetas* can be shaped and breaded then wrapped tightly, frozen, and saved for later use for up to one month.

CROQUETAS DE MEDIA NOCHE

MAKES 24 *CROQUETAS*

This recipe is inspired by the croquetas de media noche *I first had at Bread + Butter, Alberto Cabrera's Coral Gables gastropub by way of a Cuban lunch counter. Cabrera takes the elements of the traditional* media noche *sandwich—sweet ham, sharp swiss cheese, spicy yellow mustard, and pickles for punch—and blends them with a creamy béchamel sauce that is then breaded, fried, and served alongside spicy yellow mustard.*

2 tablespoons unsalted butter, cubed

1 cup plus 4 tablespoons unbleached all-purpose flour, divided

1½ cups whole milk

4 ounces cooked ham, trimmed and diced

2 ounces Swiss cheese (such as Emmentaler or Jarlsberg), finely shredded

¼ cup dill pickles, minced

1 teaspoon yellow mustard, plus more to serve

1 teaspoon kosher salt

¼ teaspoon freshly ground white pepper

4 extra-large eggs, well-beaten

2 cups panko or dried bread crumbs, finely ground, divided

Canola or peanut oil for deep frying

Melt the butter in a heavy saucepan over medium-low heat. Add 4 tablespoons of flour and cook, stirring constantly until well blended but not browned, about 2 minutes. Gradually pour in the milk and continue stirring until the sauce has thickened and the whisk leaves trace marks on the surface, 5 additional minutes. Remove the saucepan from the heat and stir in the ham, cheese, and pickles until well blended. Stir in the mustard, salt, and white pepper to taste and set aside to cool.

Pour the *croqueta* mixture into a shallow bowl. Cover the filling with plastic wrap and refrigerate until set, at least one hour or overnight.

Preheat the oven to 200°F. Line a 13 x 18 x 1-inch baking sheet with parchment paper or a nonstick liner.

Place the beaten eggs, remaining flour, and 1 cup of bread crumbs in separate mixing bowls. Lightly oil your hands and spoon the béchamel mixture into walnut-size pieces then roll into the desired shape. Dip the *croqueta* in the egg then roll in the flour, shaking off the excess by passing it between your hands 2 to 3 times. Dip the *croqueta* in the egg a second time then roll in the bread crumbs. The *croqueta* should be completely coated with bread crumbs so they do not leak when fried. Repeat with the remaining filling and replenish the bread crumbs as needed. Transfer the breaded *croquetas* to the lined baking sheet and refrigerate until ready to use.

Heat 2 inches of oil over medium heat in a deep 10-inch skillet or heavy pot until a deep-fat thermometer registers 365°F.

Carefully add the *croquetas* in batches, turning occasionally, until brown on all sides, about 2 minutes. Remove with a slotted spoon and transfer to a plate lined with paper towels then place in a baking pan in the preheated to oven to keep warm while you fry the remaining *croquetas*. Return the oil to 365°F in between batches. Serve immediately with spicy yellow mustard.

NOTE

After the *croquetas* are shaped and breaded, they can be wrapped tightly frozen and saved for later use for up to one month.

CHEF ALBERTO CABRERA'S EARLIEST
education came at his grandmother's table
where she always had a changing menu
with everyone's favorites on hand. With
family members dropping by at different
times, there were several seatings a day.
It's not surprising that Cabrera combines
classic Cuban cafeteria staples with the
thoughtful home cooking he grew up
with—from *butifarras* and head cheese to
marmalades and milk fudge.

Stuffed Potatoes

PAPAS RELLENAS

MAKES 16 LARGE OR 32 SMALL STUFFED POTATOES

It's traditional for mothers to give their daughters a copy of the classic Cuban cookbook Cocina Criolla *by famed food writer Nitza Villapol when they get married or turn twenty-five— whichever comes first. When Janice Lusky married Mark Greenspan, her mother decided to give a copy to her new son-in-law instead. Years later, they consider him thoroughly* aplatanado— *practicing his Spanish, smoking cigars, and cooking Cuban food whenever possible. In his version of classic* papas rellenas, *the picadillo is given an extra-strong dose of cumin, cinnamon, and nutmeg that stands up well to the potato filling.*

3 pounds russet potatoes, peeled and quartered

2 to 4 tablespoons heavy cream, at room temperature

1 teaspoon kosher salt

¼ teaspoon freshly ground black pepper

3 extra-large eggs beaten with 1 tablespoon of water

½ cup unbleached all-purpose flour

2 cups panko or coarse dried bread crumbs, divided

4 cups Picadillo Filling (page 43)

4 cups canola oil, plus more for shaping

Place the potatoes in a 5-quart heavy pot with water to cover by 1 inch. Bring the potatoes to a hard boil then immediately lower the heat to maintain a gentle simmer. Cover and cook the potatoes until they are tender, 15 to 20 minutes. Drain and quickly return the potatoes to the same pot, off-heat, so that any remaining moisture evaporates, 2 to 3 minutes. Run the potatoes while still warm through a food mill or ricer and place in a large mixing bowl. Gently blend in the cream, salt, and black pepper to form a smooth but firm dough (about 4 cups). Chill until ready to use.

Measure out ¼ cup of potato or use an ice-cream scoop to form a half ball in the cup of your hand. Create a well in the center of each ball and fill with 2 tablespoons of picadillo filling. Gently push the filling into the center as you close the potato dough around the filling to form a round, smooth ball.

Line a 13 x 18 x 1-inch baking sheet with parchment paper or a nonstick liner.

Place the beaten eggs, flour, and 1 cup of bread crumbs in separate mixing bowls. Dip a potato ball in the egg then roll in the flour, shaking off the excess flour by passing it between your hands 2 to 3 times. Dip the potato ball in the egg a second time then roll it in the bread crumbs. They should be completely coated with bread crumbs so they do not leak when fried. Replenish the bread crumbs as needed. Transfer to the lined baking sheet and refrigerate until ready to use, at least 2 hours.

Preheat the oven to 200°F.

Heat 2 inches of oil over medium heat in a 4-quart heavy pot until a deep-fat thermometer registers 365°F.

Carefully add the potatoes in batches, turning occasionally, until brown on all sides, 3 to 4 minutes. Remove with a slotted spoon and transfer to a plate lined with paper towels then place in a baking pan in the preheated oven to keep warm while you fry the remaining potatoes. Return the oil to 365°F in between batches. Serve immediately.

PICADILLO FILLING

MAKES 3 CUPS

¼ cup extra-virgin olive oil

1 large yellow onion, chopped

1 large cubanelle pepper (also known as Italian frying pepper), stemmed, seeded, and diced

3 large garlic cloves, minced

1 teaspoon kosher salt

¼ teaspoon freshly ground black pepper

1 pound ground beef, chuck or rump

¼ cup tomato paste

1 teaspoon ground cumin

½ teaspoon ground cinnamon

¼ teaspoon ground nutmeg

½ cup tomato purée

½ cup dry white wine

⅔ cup pimiento-stuffed olives, halved and with ¼ cup of the juice

1 to 2 tablespoons rice wine or sherry vinegar

¼ to ½ teaspoon cayenne pepper

Heat the oil in a large skillet over medium heat. Add the onion, cubanelle pepper, garlic, salt, and black pepper and sauté until the onion is translucent, 6 to 8 minutes. Raise the heat to medium-high and add the beef to brown, breaking it up so there are no lumps, about 5 minutes.

Drain off any excess fat and lower the heat to medium. Add the tomato paste, cumin, cinnamon, and nutmeg and sauté an additional 3 to 5 minutes. Stir in the tomato purée, wine, and olives with their juice. Lower the heat to maintain a gentle simmer and continue to cook until the liquid is absorbed, 10 to 15 minutes. Add the vinegar, cayenne pepper, and adjust the seasonings to taste. Bring to room temperature then use to fill *Papas Rellenas* (page 42), *Empanaditas* (page 32) or *Tostones* (page 223).

Variation: YUCA RELLENA

This recipe also works well with yuca, which can be filled then shaped into round or torpedo-shaped *croquetas*. Replace the potatoes with 3 pounds of fresh or frozen yuca cut into 2-inch chunks. Boil as directed and then slice in half and remove the fibrous core. Mash the yuca and proceed with the recipe as directed.

NOTE

The stuffed potatoes can be shaped and breaded then wrapped tightly and frozen for up to one month. If the potatoes are frozen, bring the oil to 375°F before frying.

CAFÉ CUBANO

SERVES 4 TO 6

It's impossible to imagine Cuba without coffee. Yet it wasn't until the influx of French coffee growers fleeing the Haitian revolution in the mid-eighteenth century that coffee became a viable crop on the island—most prominently around Santiago de Cuba and Guantánamo, the central province of Las Villas, and Pinar del Río, where you can still see the ruins of old French plantations. Though this initial surge was short-lived and soon after relegated to the eastern provinces where the French influence was strongest, Cuban coffee culture took root. Every visit to a Cuban home starts with the offer of un cafecito *topped with a thick layer of caramel-colored foam called the* espumita *and every night ends with a passed tray filled with thimblefuls of sweet coffee.*

Ground dark roast espresso, such as La Llave, Bustelo, or Pilon

2 tablespoons sugar or more to taste

Using a 6-cup stove top espresso maker, fill the lower chamber with cold water. Insert the funnel and fill with espresso. Pat smooth with the back of a spoon to level off but do not press down. Replace the upper chamber and screw tightly. Place the pot over low heat.

Pour the sugar into a glass measuring cup. When the coffee begins to percolate, take the first few drops and add it to the sugar. Return the pot to the heat so that it continues to percolate.

Beat the coffee and sugar vigorously with a spoon or whisk to form a pale and creamy paste. Add a few more drops of coffee if needed to incorporate all of the sugar. Pour in the remaining espresso in a steady stream and mix until well blended. Pour into the individual demitasse cups and serve.

Variation: CORTADO

Prepare a pot of freshly brewed *Café Cubano* layered with caramel foam as before. Pour into individual demitasse cups and add steamed whole milk or evaporated milk to taste.

Variation: CAFÉ CON LECHE

Prepare a pot of freshly brewed *Café Cubano* layered with caramel foam as before and combine with one cup of steamed whole milk.

EL PECADO

MAKES 1

When you first walk into Tinta y Café, it's hard not to focus on how different it is from the typical ventanita. A family business run by Malu Statz and her cousin Carlos Santamarina, here the sandwiches are well-pressed but made with freshly baked French baguettes, the empanadas are Argentinian, and Colombian sancocho *is as likely a daily special as Cuban* tamal en cazuela. *Drawing in people from both its historic little Havana neighborhood and upscale Brickell nearby, what hasn't changed is the sound—the steady murmur of customers crowding the sidewalk that streams in through the open window and wraps itself around the lunch counter where regulars place their orders and make themselves heard over the ever-playing music and steady din from the kitchen. Their* el pecado, *layered with condensed milk, espresso, steamed evaporated milk, and topped with the perfect milky foam, turns coffee into dessert—a forgivable sin.*

2 tablespoons sweetened condensed milk

4 ounces prepared *Café Cubano* (page 45) or freshly brewed espresso

¼ cup evaporated milk

¼ cup whole milk

Fill the bottom of an 8-ounce glass with condensed milk.

Slowly pour the espresso over the condensed milk to create a second layer. Bring the evaporated milk to a simmer in a small saucepan, then pour into the espresso layer. Simmer the whole milk then whisk until frothy. Top off the glass with the beaten whole milk.

SITTING AROUND THE
LUNCH COUNTER

Beginning in the 1930s, in both Cuba and Cuban enclaves in South Florida, twenty-four-
hour sandwich counters and propane-fueled carts selling spice-filled burgers called
fritas were convenient street food for people unable to make it home for lunch or
late-night revelers not ready to make it home just yet.

Their popularity has only grown in Miami where baptisms and funerals, *quinces*
and weddings, concerts and baseball games typically end at fifties-style chrome-
edged tabletops and wraparound counters set with paper placemat menus. Cuban
cafeterias serve up expertly pressed sandwiches, fritters, tropical fruit shakes, and
icy *guarapo* (sugarcane juice). At the center of it all is the *lonchero*—an apron-clad
conductor in kitchen whites holding a long serrated bread knife in one hand and a
pronged fork in the other, carving out slices of sweet ham and marinated pork to
pack into pale loaves of Cuban bread.

Brightly lit and starkly utilitarian, these lunch counters inspire genuine follow-
ings. Looking through a stack of old menus and advertisements from the early 1960s
at the University of Miami's Cuban Heritage Collection, I realized why. Apart from
authentic Creole home cooking, each new place offered the chance of seeing people
you knew, making these impermanent stalls and carts brick-and-mortar points of
reunion.

SANDWICH CUBANO | *cuban sandwich* . . . 53

MEDIA NOCHE | *midnight sandwich* . . . 57

PAN CON LECHÓN | *roast pork sandwich* . . . 60

FRITAS A CABALLO CON PAPITAS A LA JULIANA | *cuban-style hamburgers with shoestring fries* . . . 63

SANDWICH ELENA RUZ . . . 65

PAN CON MINUTA | *breaded fish sandwich* . . . 68

BOLLITOS DE CARITA | *black-eyed pea fritters* . . . 73

MARIQUITAS CON VINAGRETA DE CILANTRO Y LIMÓN | *plantain chips with lime-cilantro vinaigrette* . . . 74

BATIDOS | *tropical fruit shakes: mamey, mango, soursop* . . . 77

Cuban Sandwich

SANDWICH CUBANO

MAKES 4

This recipe comes from my uncle Victor Pujals, who has given considerable thought to engineering the perfect Cubano. *Fill the sandwich with slightly more ham than shredded pork—either a lean cut of pork loin or well-trimmed roasted pork—and cover the bread from* rabo a cabo, *or end to end. Allow the Swiss cheese to peek out of the sides so that it crisps up on the hot press as it melts, spread the mustard thinly, and use the sliced pickles sparingly.*

2 large loaves Pan de Agua (page 311), cut in half to make 4 pieces, and sliced lengthwise

4 tablespoons yellow mustard

12 ounces sweet-cured ham, thickly sliced and at room temperature

8 ounces Lechón Asado (page 169) sliced, trimmed of any excess fat, and at room temperature

4 ounces Swiss cheese (Emmentaler or Jarlsberg), thinly sliced

2 large dill pickles, thinly sliced crosswise

4 tablespoons (½ stick) butter, softened, plus more for greasing

Spread both sides of each bread loaf with mustard. Layer the bottom half with ham, pork, and cheese to cover the bread from end to end. Top with sliced pickles to taste. Brush the outside of the bread, both top and bottom, with butter.

Heat a sandwich press over medium heat. Lightly brush the inside of the press with additional butter. Press the sandwich until the cheese is melted and the meats are warm, 4 to 5 minutes.

Alternately, heat a 12-inch cast-iron skillet over medium heat. Create a press by wrapping a brick, heavy skillet, or can of soup in aluminum foil. Place the sandwich in the skillet and press down on the sandwich, turning once, until it is warmed through and the outside crust is golden, 2 to 3 minutes per side. Repeat with the remaining sandwiches. Slice on the diagonal and serve.

Variation: TAMPA-STYLE SANDWICH CUBANO

Prepare the sandwich and add 4 ounces of thinly sliced Genoa salami in between the meat and cheese layer. Proceed as directed.

Variation: CROQUETA PREPARADA

Prepare the sandwich and add 2 *Croquetas de Jamón* (page 36) in between the meat and cheese layer. Proceed as directed.

A DESCENDANT OF THE SPANISH MIXTO sandwich or *sandwich en pan de flauta,* the *Sandwich Cubano* only became Cuban when it left the island. Favored by sugar-mill and cigar-factory workers who migrated between Cuba and Key West in the late nineteenth century, they brought the sandwich with them when Vicente Martínez Ybor moved his Principe de Gales cigar operation from Key West to Tampa in 1885. When they began working alongside Italian immigrants, Genoa salami was added to the *mixto* of sugar-cured pork, ham, and cheese that is still part of the traditional Tampa Cubano served in Ybor City. In Havana, where it was a popular item at restaurants and cafés in the 1930s, it was slathered in butter and heated in a flat sandwich press called a *plancha.* With the influx of more recent arrivals from Cuba, the pressed version became a standby at Florida lunch counters, but it's only the beginning. Layer in a couple of *croquetas de jamón* and it becomes a *croqueta preparada,* or substitute pale loaves of *pan de agua* with a sweet bread roll for a *media noche.* The Cuban Sandwich has many claimants, so it's not surprising everyone has an opinion on how to go about putting one together.

MEDIA NOCHE

MAKES 4

The Cubano's cuter cousin, the Media Noche *was sold as a late-night snack in Havana's cafés. Calling for the same blend of sweet-cured ham, Swiss cheese, and pickles, it works best with juicier cuts of pork—though what really sets it apart is the egg-rich* Pan de Media Noche *(page 300).*

4 large rolls Pan de Media Noche (page 300), or sweet roll-like brioche or challah, sliced lengthwise

4 tablespoons yellow mustard

12 ounces sweet-cured ham, thickly sliced

8 ounces Lechón Asado (page 169) or Masas de Puerco (page 172), sliced, trimmed of any excess fat, and at room temperature

4 ounces Swiss cheese (Emmentaler or Jarlsberg), thinly sliced

2 large dill pickles, thinly sliced crosswise

4 tablespoons (½ stick) butter, melted and cooled to room temperature, plus more for greasing

Spread both sides of each roll with mustard. Layer the bottom half with ham, pork, and cheese to cover the bread from end to end. Top with sliced pickles to taste. Brush the outside of the bread, both top and bottom, with butter.

Heat a sandwich press over medium heat. Lightly brush the inside of the press with additional butter. Press the sandwich until the cheese is melted and the meats are warm, 3 to 5 minutes.

Alternately, heat a 12-inch cast-iron skillet over medium heat. Create a press by wrapping a brick, heavy skillet, or can of soup in aluminum foil. Place the sandwich in the skillet and press down on the sandwich, turning once, until it is warmed through and the outside crust is golden, 2 to 3 minutes per side. Repeat with the remaining sandwiches. Slice on the diagonal and serve.

Variation: MEDIO DIAS | MIDDAY SANDWICHES

Replace the larger rolls with 12 small *Pan de Media Noche* rolls. Redistribute the same amount of filling over the smaller rolls and serve. They do not have to be buttered or pressed.

Roast Pork Sandwich

PAN CON LECHÓN

MAKES 4

With its airy texture and subtle lard flavor, a lightly toasted pan de manteca *is the perfect vehicle for leftover* Lechón Asado *(page 169), drenched in* mojo, *and smothered in onions.*

2 whole loaves Pan de Manteca (page 299) or Italian lard bread, cut in half to make 4 pieces and sliced lengthwise

¼ cup olive oil

16 ounces Lechón Asado (page 169), sliced and trimmed of any excess fat

1 cup freshly prepared Mojo Criollo (page 301)

1 large yellow onion, thinly sliced

4 ripe tomatoes, sliced

Slice each loaf in half lengthwise. Lightly brush the inside with olive oil and place facedown on a dry skillet to toast, 1 to 2 minutes total.

Layer the bottom half of the toasted bread with pork from end to end. Top with onions and tomato. Drizzle with 3 to 4 tablespoons of the prepared *mojo* and top with remaining bread. Cut on the diagonal and serve.

Cuban-style Hamburgers with Shoestring Fries

FRITAS A CABALLO CON PAPITAS A LA JULIANA

MAKES 12 PATTIES

Victoriano Benito González started his first frita *stand in Placetas, Las Villas, when he was just twelve years old. He shouldn't have been surprised that his daughter Mercedes wanted to spend all her time at his cafeteria,* El Rey de las Fritas, *a Little Havana fixture since the 1970s. Over his objections, Mercedes would have the school bus drop her off there so she could spend the afternoon chatting up customers, hiding under the tables, and stealing fries. Working alongside him, she learned how to run the restaurant to his standards. The family zealously guards the secret to their* frita *recipe, but Mercedes offered a few suggestions for the perfect* frita—*pointing me toward adding chorizo to the patty mixture and away from bread crumbs. They also reserve a small amount of their special sauce to drizzle on top of the patties as they are mashed into the griddle, making them well-done, but never dry. All the better to make room for the freshly fried potatoes piled on top.*

FOR THE SAUCE

4 tablespoons olive oil, plus more as
    needed

1 medium yellow onion, chopped

4 large garlic cloves, chopped

2 teaspoons smoked *pimentón*
    (Spanish-style paprika)

1 teaspoon ground cumin

1 teaspoon kosher salt

¼ teaspoon freshly ground black pepper

2 tablespoons tomato paste

1 cup beef stock or water

2 tablespoons white wine vinegar

1 to 2 tablespoons Worcestershire sauce to
    taste

FOR THE PATTIES

1 pound ground beef chuck

½ pound ground pork

½ pound semi-cured Spanish chorizo,
    casings removed, and cut into 1-inch
    chunks

12 small potato hamburger rolls

To make the sauce, heat 2 tablespoons of olive oil in a 10-inch heavy skillet over medium heat. Add the onion, garlic, *pimentón*, cumin, salt, and black pepper and cook until the onion is soft and translucent, about 5 minutes. Add the tomato paste and work into the onions until well blended. Stir in the water, vinegar, and Worcestershire sauce to taste and simmer an additional 5 minutes. Allow the sauce to cool slightly, then pour into a food processor or blender and pulse until it is smooth and pourable (about 1½ cups).

To make the patties, combine the beef, pork, chorizo, and ¾ cup of the prepared sauce in a food processor and pulse until just combined—do not overwork—1 to 2 minutes. Set aside the meat mixture and reserve the remaining sauce.

Shape the meat mixture into 12 patties, ½ inch thick. Rest the patties in the refrigerator for 1 hour to allow the flavors to develop.

Heat the remaining 2 tablespoons of olive oil in the skillet over medium heat. Working in batches, add the patties to the pan. As they cook, flatten the patties with a metal spatula and cover each patty with a teaspoon of the reserved sauce. Turn and repeat on the other side until they reach the desired degree of doneness, 2 to 4 minutes on each side. Replenish the oil as needed. Serve on warmed rolls with fried eggs and shoestring fries.

PAPAS FRITAS A LA JULIANA | SHOESTRING FRIES
MAKES 6 CUPS

1½ pounds russet potatoes, peeled

3 cups peanut or canola oil

Sea salt for sprinkling

Using a mandolin or food processor fitted with a julienne disc, cut the potatoes lengthwise into strips about ⅛ inch thick. Soak the potatoes in water until ready to use. Drain the potatoes in a colander then rinse them thoroughly until the water runs clear. Pat the potatoes dry with paper towels before frying to avoid oil splatter. Heat the oil over medium-high heat in a 4-quart heavy pot until a deep-fat thermometer registers 375°F.

Fry the potatoes in small batches until golden, 2 to 4 minutes. Transfer the potatoes to a plate lined with paper towels. Return the oil to 375°F in between batches and repeat with the remaining potatoes. Sprinkle the potatoes while still warm with sea salt to taste.

SANDWICH ELENA RUZ

MAKES 4

The Elena Ruz sandwich always seemed a little out of place on the menu. A combination of roasted turkey, cream cheese, and strawberry preserves, it floats alongside the heavier ham-pork-cheese sandwiches—lighter and prettier with a first and last name. It was named for Elena Ruz, a Havana socialite who had this unusual combination made to order for her at El Carmelo, a fashionable café in the 1930s. Eventually, it landed on the menu and became a popular item. According to later interviews, her parents were scandalized to see a sign for "Sandwich Elena Ruz 25 centavos" on display, though, as she pointed out, the other sandwiches only went for ten cents.

4 large rolls Pan de Media Noche (page 300) or sweet roll-like brioche or challah, sliced lengthwise

4 tablespoons strawberry preserves

12 ounces roasted turkey, thickly sliced

4 tablespoons cream cheese, softened

4 tablespoons (½ stick) unsalted butter, plus more for greasing

Spread both sides of each roll with an even layer of strawberry preserves. Cover with a layer of roasted turkey and top with an even layer of cream cheese.

Brush the outside of the bread, both top and bottom, with butter. Heat a sandwich press over medium heat. Lightly brush the inside of the press with additional butter. Press the sandwich until it is lightly toasted and warmed through, 2 to 3 minutes total.

Alternately, heat a 12-inch cast-iron skillet over medium heat. Create a press by wrapping a brick, heavy skillet, or can of soup in aluminum foil. Place the sandwich in the skillet and press down on the sandwich, turning once, until it is warmed through and the outside crust is lightly toasted, 2 to 3 minutes total. Repeat with the remaining sandwiches. Slice on the diagonal and serve.

Latin American

Bocadito Preparado
White Bread Sandwich $5.15

Galleta Preparada
Cracker Sandwich $4.75

Croqueta Surtida $6.65

Croqueta Preparada $5.60

Tuna Sandwich
Tuna $5.45

Tamal Tamale $5.45

Croqueta Croquette
Regular "Alfredo" $4.75

Especial $6.95

Frita "Alberto" $3.45

De Bacon Bacon Sandwich $4.00

Club sandwich $8.00

Minuta Fish Sandwich $6.00

Media Noche Midnight $5.00

Media Noche de Pierna $5.00

Serrano Surtido Regular
White Ham Regular $7.45

Serrano Surtido Especial
Ham Special $8.45

$5.35

Breaded Fish Sandwich

PAN CON MINUTA

MAKES 4 SANDWICHES

This pan con minuta *is inspired by the sandwich served in Little Havana's La Camaronera.* *Topped with a spicy tomato* sofrito *and* Bollitos de Carita *(page 73) on the side, you can almost imagine you're standing elbow to elbow at their popular lunch counter.*

FOR THE *MINUTAS*

Four 5-ounce snapper fillets or other white-fleshed fish, skinned

¼ cup freshly squeezed lime juice

Sea salt

Freshly ground black pepper

2 cups unbleached all-purpose flour

1 cup cracker meal or bread crumbs, finely ground

1 teaspoon sea salt

¼ teaspoon freshly ground black pepper

2 cups peanut or canola oil

FOR THE TOMATO *SOFRITO*

2 tablespoons extra-virgin olive oil

1 medium yellow onion, diced

½ large green bell pepper, stemmed, seeded, and diced

½ large red bell pepper, stemmed, seeded, and diced

2 large garlic cloves, minced

1 teaspoon sea salt

¼ teaspoon freshly ground black pepper

1 cup Tomato Purée (page 304) or canned tomato purée

¼ cup dry white wine

2 tablespoons freshly squeezed lemon or lime juice

1 dried bay leaf

4 Pan de Agua rolls (page 311) or soft sandwich roll

To make the *minutas*, place the fillets in a large glass baking dish. Pour the lime juice over the fillets then sprinkle with salt and pepper. Cover the dish and chill in the refrigerator, 30 to 60 minutes.

Combine the flour, cracker meal, sea salt, and black pepper in a medium mixing bowl. Spread 1 cup of the flour mixture on a plate. Remove the fillets from the marinade and coat in the flour mixture, brushing off the excess. Replenish the flour mixture as needed. Refrigerate the coated fillets until ready to use and prepare the *sofrito*.

To prepare the *sofrito*, heat the olive oil in a 10-inch skillet. Add the onion, green and red peppers, garlic, salt, and black pepper and sauté until the onion is soft and translucent, 6 to 8 minutes. Add the tomato purée, wine, juice and bay leaf and bring to a simmer. Simmer covered over low heat for 10 to 15 minutes. Adjust the seasonings to taste.

Heat the peanut oil in a heavy 10-inch skillet over medium-high heat until hot but not smoking. Working in batches, add the coated fillets to the skillet and fry until golden brown on both sides, 3 to 4 minutes. Transfer the fillets to a plate lined with paper towels until ready to use.

Split each sandwich roll. Place a fillet on the bottom of the roll and top with the prepared *sofrito* to taste. Top the roll and serve.

AS THE ONLY SEASICK BROTHER IN A LARGE family of fishermen, Mario García was left to prepare the catch his brothers' brought in to sell from their fish-fry stand in the port city of Cárdenas. When their boats were confiscated soon after the revolution, the brothers kept to fishing, gradually finding their way to Miami. In 1966, Mario, together with his brothers Arsenio, Juan, Felix, Ramón, and Esteban, opened their own fish market in Little Havana named La Camaronera. Eventually, they added a stand-up seafood counter best known for Mario's *pan con minuta*—snapper fillets served up with the tail still on as though the fish jumped out of the ocean already breaded and landed on a soft Cuban bread roll. Now David and Maritza García have taken over the day-to-day operations from their fathers, who appear once in a while to make sure it's all going smoothly. Their boats still bring in fresh fish every day and the menu has hardly changed, but what started as a business of brothers has become about cousins.

BOLLITOS DE CARITA

MAKES 16 FRITTERS

Black-eyed pea fritters are often associated with Chinese vendors who sold them in the streets of Havana. In Miami, they're a favorite at La Camaronera, where they are made to order. Owner Maritza García walked me through the process, which starts with the beans being passed through an ancient grinder, then peeled by hand, soaked, and lightly seasoned to form a loose batter that puffs up when it is dropped into the fryer. For small batches, a spice or coffee grinder can be used to crack the peas so that skins easily pull away when they are run under cold water.

½ pound dried black-eyed peas

⅓ cup water, plus more as needed

4 large garlic cloves, peeled

1 teaspoon kosher salt

¼ teaspoon freshly ground white pepper

3 cups canola oil or peanut oil for frying

Place the dried beans in a grain mill or coffee grinder and pulse until roughly crushed, 2 to 3 times. Transfer the beans to a large mixing bowl and flush with cold water, rinsing thoroughly until the spotted skins separate and rise to the top. Remove the skins with a skimmer or small sieve and repeat until the beans are peeled and mostly white.

Strain the beans and place them in the same bowl with fresh water to cover. Soak the beans until they are tripled in volume, 3 to 4 hours. Line a colander with cheesecloth and drain until completely dry, at least 2 hours or overnight.

Combine the beans, garlic, water, salt, and white pepper in a food processor and pulse briefly to combine. Add more water if needed. The batter should be creamy but textured and mound easily on a spoon.

Heat 2 inches of oil over medium heat in a 4-quart heavy pot or deep fryer until a deep-fat thermometer registers 375°F.

Working in batches, carefully drop the batter in rounded tablespoons until they are browned and float to the top, 3 to 4 minutes. Remove the fritters with a slotted spoon and transfer to a plate lined with paper towels. Return the oil to 375°F in between batches and repeat with remaining batter.

Fried Plantains with Lime-Cilantro Vinaigrette

MARIQUITAS CON VINAGRETA DE CILANTRO Y LIMÓN

MAKES 4 CUPS

Once the order is placed, mariquitas cannot hit the table fast enough, and they never last long. Peeled off into ribbonlike shavings, the plantains crisp the moment they hit the oil, going gold as they slide along the surface.

3 large green plantains
2 cups canola or grapeseed oil

Sea salt

Run each plantain under warm water before peeling. Using a sharp knife, trim the ends and score each plantain lengthwise along the peel. Remove the peel in sections.

Using a vegetable peeler, pare each plantain lengthwise into 5-inch shavings. If not frying immediately, the shavings can be placed in a bowl and covered with cold water and 1 tablespoon of lime juice. Drain and pat dry with paper towels before frying.

Heat the oil in a heavy 10-inch skillet to 365°F. Add the slices to the oil 5 to 6 at a time, turning them until they are crisp, 1 to 2 minutes. Do not overcrowd the skillet. Transfer the plantains to a plate lined with paper towels. Sprinkle with sea salt while still warm and serve with *Lime-Cilantro Vinaigrette* (see recipe below).

LIME-CILANTRO VINAIGRETTE

MAKES 4 CUPS

4 large garlic cloves, peeled
2 tablespoons freshly squeezed lime juice
1 teaspoon Dijón mustard
1 teaspoon sea salt

¼ teaspoon freshly ground black pepper
½ cup extra-virgin olive oil
¼ cup fresh cilantro, finely chopped

Combine the garlic, lime juice, mustard, sea salt, and black pepper in a food processor and pulse until it forms a smooth paste. With the motor running, slowly add the olive oil in a steady stream until smooth. Whisk in the fresh cilantro and adjust the seasonings to taste.

Variation: CHICHARRITAS | PLANTAIN CHIPS

Peel the plantains. Using a sharp knife or mandoline, slice the plantains crosswise into chips about ⅛ inch thick. Proceed as directed.

BATIDOS

Cuban-American artist Luis Gispert is always sending friends black-and-white images of the sleepy town Miami we all grew up in. The flavors of the tropical batidos he whips up at home, however, are pure Technicolor.

BATIDO DE MAMEY | MAMEY SHAKE

MAKES 1 SHAKE

2 cups ripe mamey, fresh or frozen, cut into 1-inch chunks

1 cup cold whole milk or evaporated milk

1 cup crushed ice

Sugar

Combine the ingredients in the jar of a blender and process at the highest speed until frothy. Add sugar to taste. Serve in a chilled glass.

BATIDO DE MANGO | MANGO SHAKE

MAKES 1 SHAKE

2 cups ripe mangos, fresh or frozen, peeled and cut into 1-inch chunks

1 cup cold whole milk or evaporated milk

1 cup crushed ice

¼ cup sweetened condensed milk

Pinch of salt

Sugar

Combine the ingredients in the jar of a blender and process at the highest speed until frothy. Add sugar to taste. Serve in a chilled glass.

BATIDO DE GUANÁBANA | SOURSOP SHAKE

MAKES 1 SHAKE

2 cups *guanábana* (also known as soursop), fresh or frozen, cut into 1-inch chunks

1 cup cold whole milk or evaporated milk

1 cup crushed ice

Sugar

Combine the ingredients in the jar of a blender and process at the highest speed until frothy. Add sugar to taste. Serve in a chilled glass.

SOUPS and STEWS

In the beginning, there was ajiaco: a rich stew of native corn, yuca, boniato, and meats with pre-Columbian roots stretching back to the island's indigenous Taíno population. Ajiaco gets its name from the hot *ajíes* once used before they gave way to sweeter varieties. The Spanish added cuts of pork and a cured beef called *tasajo* to the pot, but the recipe wasn't complete until Africans introduced plantains and tubers such as *ñame* and *malanga*. It wasn't an overstatement when anthropologist Fernando Ortiz compared Cuba to an *ajiaco* put to the fire of the tropics. It's a history that repeats itself in countless recipes that embody the push and pull of Spanish and African traditions—an *ajiaco* of flavors that are always at a boil.

In the countryside where many of these recipes were developed, a heavy midday stew sustained you through a long day's labors. Until the early 1960s, Cubans observed the Spanish siesta when parents and children went home in the afternoon to enjoy large family lunches before returning to work or school. You could never be sure which siblings, aunts, uncles, cousins, or neighbors might join you, so a little more broth, a slower simmer, and a few added vegetables in the pot ensured you always had enough. Soothing *crema de malanga*, tender corn dumplings added to a pot of *quimbombó*, or smoke-filled *caldo gallego* became well-loved parts of every Cuban meal. The ritual was repeated in the evening, so a well-seasoned stew could be served as a first course at lunch then become a meal in and of itself at night. Cooked over several hours or quickly pressurized for weekday meals, these soups and stews exemplify the Cuban cooks' love of improvisation.

CREMA DE MALANGA | *cream of malanga soup* . . . 83

SOPA DE AJO CON HUEVOS | *garlic soup with poached eggs* . . . 84

SOPA DE PLÁTANO | *plantain soup* . . . 86

SOPA DE DE POLLO CON FIDEOS | *chicken noodle soup* . . . 87

TAMAL EN CAZUELA | *tamal in a pot* . . . 89

SOPA DE LENTEJAS CON PLÁTANOS MADUROS | *lentil soup with ripe plantains* . . . 93

PESCADO EN SALSA DE PERRO CAIBARIÉN | *fish and leek soup* . . . 94

QUIMBOMBÓ CON BOLITAS DE PLÁTANO | *okra stew with plantain dumplings* . . . 96

CALDO GALLEGO | *galician stew* . . . 102

AJIACO CRIOLLO CON CASABE | *creole stew with yuca flatbread* . . . 105

Cream of Malanga Soup

CREMA DE MALANGA

SERVES 4

Crema de Malanga *is typically given to the youngest and oldest members of the family. For everyone in between, it's a cure-all when you're not feeling well and comfort food when you are.*

2 pounds white malanga (also known as yautía), peeled and quartered

1 cup Chicken Stock (page 306), or store-bought chicken stock (optional)

Sea salt

Freshly ground white pepper

2 tablespoons extra-virgin oil

Place the malanga in a 5-quart heavy pot with enough water to cover by 1 inch. Bring to a boil over medium heat then cover and simmer until tender, 15 to 20 minutes. Drain the malanga and reserve the cooking water.

Place the malanga in a food processor and purée until smooth. Add a small amount of cooking water as needed to reach the desired texture. Return to the pot and simmer over low heat until warmed through. For a thinner soup, stir in the chicken broth. Add the sea salt and white pepper to taste. Drizzle with olive oil and serve.

Garlic Soup with Poached Eggs

SOPA DE AJO CON HUEVOS

SERVES 6

This very Spanish soup is served in Cuban households to counterbalance a heavy midday meal. The bread is fried in garlic-infused oil while a large dose of pimentón *makes this Spartan soup anything but plain.*

¼ cup extra-virgin olive oil

8 large garlic cloves, peeled and lightly crushed with the back of knife

6 slices country-style white bread

6 cups Chicken Stock (page 306), or store-bought chicken stock

1 teaspoon *pimentón* (Spanish smoked paprika)

1 teaspoon sea salt

¼ teaspoon freshly ground black pepper

6 large eggs

Fresh flat-leaf parsley, leaves and tender stems, finely chopped (optional)

Heat the oil over medium heat in a 5-quart heavy pot. Add the mashed garlic cloves and sauté until lightly golden on all sides, 1 to 2 minutes. Remove the garlic cloves from the oil and reserve.

Working in batches, fry the bread over medium heat until lightly golden, 2 to 3 minutes. Remove the fried bread and cut into 1-inch pieces. Set aside until ready to use.

Add the chicken stock to the pot and bring to a fast simmer over medium heat, about 5 minutes. Using a mortar and pestle, mash the reserved garlic, *pimentón*, sea salt, and black pepper to a paste. Add the garlic paste to the broth, adjust the seasonings to taste, and return to a simmer.

Crack the eggs into a cup or saucer and slide into the soup. Simmer the eggs until the whites set, 3 to 4 minutes. Distribute the bread into individual bowls. Ladle the hot soup over the bread and top with a poached egg. Sprinkle with freshly chopped parsley, if using, *pimentón*, sea salt, and ground black pepper to taste. Serve immediately.

Plantain Soup

SOPA DE PLÁTANO

SERVES 4

Sopa de Plátano, *thickened with crisp, freshly fried plantains and brightened with lime juice, is a quick, improvised soup that will become a weekday favorite.*

4 cups unsalted Mariquitas or Chicharritas (page 311), plus more to garnish

4 cups Beef Stock (page 306), or store-bought beef stock

Sea salt

¼ teaspoon freshly ground black pepper

Fresh culantro, finely chopped

Lime wedges

Place the fried plantains in a food processor and pulse until it forms a coarse meal.

Pour the beef stock into a 3- to 4-quart saucepan and bring to a simmer over medium heat. Slowly add the plantain meal, stirring constantly, until the soup thickens, 3 to 5 minutes. Allow the soup to cool slightly and purée the soup using an immersion blender or blender until smooth. Rewarm the soup over low heat and season with sea salt and black pepper to taste. Garnish with fresh culantro and sprinkle with lime juice.

Chicken Noodle Soup

SOPA DE POLLO CON FIDEOS

SERVES 4 TO 6

In this sweet and sour Sopa de Pollo, *delicate Moorish noodles called* fideos *are simmered in a rich homemade chicken stock tinged with saffron.*

2 tablespoons extra-virgin olive oil

2 carrots, peeled and cut into 1-inch rounds

½ pound russet potatoes, peeled and cubed

1 small yellow onion, diced

4 garlic cloves, peeled and minced

6 cups chicken stock (page 306) or store-bought chicken stock

1 dried bay leaf

1 teaspoon kosher salt

¼ teaspoon freshly ground black pepper

½ teaspoon saffron threads

6 ounces *fideo* noodles or thin spaghetti-like noodles, such as vermicelli or spaghettini, broken up into 2-inch pieces

4 cups shredded poached chicken (page 319) or rotisserie chicken

Juice of 1 lime plus more to serve

Fresh parsley, finely chopped

To make the soup, heat the oil in a heavy 6-quart pot. Add the carrots, potatoes, onion, and garlic, and cook until the vegetables soften, about 10 minutes. Add the chicken stock, bay leaf, salt, black pepper, and saffron and bring to a fast simmer over medium heat, about 5 minutes. Add the *fideos* and continue to simmer until the noodles are tender and the vegetables are cooked through, an additional 8 to 10 minutes. Add the shredded chicken and simmer until warmed through, 3 to 5 minutes. Adjust the seasonings to taste. Sprinkle with lime juice and garnish with chopped parsley.

Tamal in a Pot

TAMAL EN CAZUELA

SERVES 4

Lilliam Domínguez Palenzuela offers a largely pan-European menu at La Cocina de Lilliam, but this traditional Tamal en Cazuela *was my favorite, and she shared the recipe with me. Fresh corn kernels are ground to a textured meal then strained to produce a milky white liquid that is blended with the onions, garlic, and tomato. A barely sweet boniato purée adds to the stew's impossibly cloudlike texture.*

6 ears field or dent corn, shucked and
    kernels cut off the cob (about 4 cups)

1 cup water

½ large white onion, quartered

4 garlic cloves

¼ pound tocino or slab bacon, diced into
    ¼-inch pieces

1 tablespoon extra-virgin olive oil

1 tablespoon unsalted butter

1 large plum tomato, seeded and diced

2 cups Chicken Stock (page 306), or
    store-bought chicken stock

3 tablespoons heavy cream

1 tablespoon turbinado sugar

1 teaspoon kosher salt

¼ teaspoon ground white pepper

Combine the corn kernels and water in a food processor and purée until it forms a textured meal. Pass the corn mixture through a fine-mesh sieve, pushing down on the corn with a wooden spoon or spatula to extract as much of the milky liquid as possible, about 2 cups. Discard the solids. Set the corn milk aside until ready to use.

Combine the onion and garlic in a food processor and pulse to form a paste. Heat the *tocino* or bacon in a 5- to 6-quart, heavy-bottom pot over medium heat until the bacon is lightly browned and has rendered its fat, 3 to 5 minutes. Add the olive oil and butter to the same pot and stir until the butter is melted. Stir in the prepared garlic paste and tomato and cook an additional 3 to 5 minutes. Stir in the chicken stock, heavy cream, sugar, salt, and white pepper and bring to a simmer. Pour in the extracted corn liquid and continue to stir over low heat until it thickens slightly, 5 to 10 minutes. Add a dollop of the prepared *Crema de Boniato* to the soup before serving.

CREMA DE BONIATO

SERVES 4

1 pound white boniato (also known as batata), peeled and quartered

2 tablespoons heavy cream

2 tablespoons extra-virgin olive oil

1 teaspoon sherry vinegar

1 teaspoon kosher salt

½ teaspoon freshly ground white pepper

Place the boniato in a 5-quart heavy pot with enough water to cover by 1 inch. Bring to a boil over medium heat, then cover and simmer until tender, 15 to 20 minutes. Drain the boniato and reserve the cooking water.

Place the boniato in a food processor and purée until smooth. Pour in the heavy cream, olive oil, vinegar, salt, and white pepper and pulse until well incorporated. Add a small amount of cooking water as needed to reach the desired texture. Set aside until ready to use.

NOTE

Fresh field or dent corn that has been preground to make tamales and stew can be found at many Latin American markets. The corn milk can be extracted one day before and kept refrigerated until ready to use. Standard American yellow corn can be substituted but is sweeter and has a higher water content. If using, combine the corn milk with ½ cup of dry, finely ground cornmeal and add to the broth in a steady stream, stirring constantly so that no lumps form. Omit the added sugar.

Lentil Soup with Ripe Plantains

SOPA DE LENTEJAS CON PLÁTANOS MADUROS

SERVES 4 TO 6

When making the rounds of friends and family's homes on New Year's Day, you're often presented with a small bowl of lentils, which are considered good luck. This Sopa de Lentejas *comes from my friend's mother Delia Vergel—a tiny force of nature who recites recipes and proverbs in the same breath and answers every question before you can think to ask. I loved her idea of browning the pork and preparing the* sofrito *inside a pressure cooker then simmering it sealed for just a few minutes to produce tender chunks that can then be added to tamales, rice dishes, and soups. Her addition of ripe yellow plantains ensures a sweet start to the new year.*

1 pound dried lentils, rinsed well

¼ cup extra-virgin olive oil

½ pound pork shoulder, cut into 1-inch chunks

½ large yellow onion, diced

½ large green bell pepper, stemmed, cored, seeded, and diced

4 large garlic cloves, peeled and diced

1 large tomato, diced

1 teaspoon kosher salt

1 teaspoon dried oregano

¼ teaspoon ground cumin

¼ teaspoon freshly ground black pepper

1 cup Tomato Purée (page 304), or canned tomato purée

1 ripe yellow plantain with black spots, peeled and cut into 1-inch slices

Place the lentils in a heavy pot with 6 cups of water. Bring to a boil then lower the heat to medium and simmer uncovered until the lentils are just tender, checking regularly and skimming the foam that forms on the top, about 10 to 15 minutes.

In the meantime, prepare the *sofrito*. Heat the oil in a 5- to 6-quart pressure cooker over medium-high heat. Add the pork and cook until lightly browned on all sides, 2 to 3 minutes. Add the onion, green pepper, and garlic and sauté until the onion is soft and translucent, 6 to 8 minutes. Add the diced tomato, salt, oregano, cumin, and black pepper and cook an additional 2 minutes. Stir in the tomato purée. Close and seal the pressure cooker and cook over medium heat for 10 to 15 minutes. Put the pressure cooker under cold running water. Do not remove the lid until the pressure comes down completely per manufacturer's instructions.

Add the lentils with their liquid to the pressure cooker with the *sofrito*. Bring to a simmer and add the plantains. Cook uncovered over medium heat until the plantains are tender and the soup is thickened, 10 to 15 minutes. Adjust the seasonings to taste and serve with pieces of fried bread.

Fish and Leek Soup

PESCADO EN SALSA DE PERRO CAIBARIÉN

SERVES 4

It seems that everyone has a story about where and how this well-known soup from the coastal town of Caibarién was invented, and it is possible at least some of them are telling the truth. The most likely story is that disappointed fishermen came back empty-handed and used whatever ingredients they had available. In this version, the leeks are simmered slowly to draw out every last drop of sweetness, an herb sachet and lime peel flavors the broth, and the potatoes are cooked until tender without disappearing altogether. It's a recipe that rewards invention.

Four 5-ounce white-flesh fish steaks or fillets, such as snapper or grouper

¼ cup extra-virgin olive oil, plus more if needed

3 large leeks, white and light green parts only, well-rinsed and sliced

1 small bunch fresh flat-leaf parsley

2 sprigs fresh oregano

1 dried bay leaf

4 large garlic cloves, peeled

1 teaspoon kosher salt

½ teaspoon freshly ground white pepper

2 medium yellow onions, chopped

1 small hot pepper, such as habanero or Scotch bonnet, stemmed, seeded, and minced

4 cups Fish Stock (page 307), or store-bought fish stock

2 medium red potatoes, scrubbed and sliced into ¼-inch rounds

One 2-inch strip of lime peel

Lime juice to taste

Pat the fish dry and sprinkle lightly with salt and freshly ground white pepper to cover. Heat the olive oil over medium-high heat in a 5- to 6-quart heavy pot or deep saucepan. Lightly sear the fish for 2 to 3 minutes on each side then set aside.

Replenish the oil if needed and add the leeks to the pot. Sauté the leeks over medium heat until they are soft and translucent but not browned, 8 to 10 minutes.

In the meantime, trim the parsley at approximately 1 inch above the stems, reserving the tender leaves for garnish. Tie the parsley stems, oregano, and bay leaf together with kitchen string to create a sachet and set aside. Using a mortar and pestle, mash together the garlic, salt, and white pepper to form a smooth paste.

Add the onions and garlic mixture to the leeks and sauté an additional 5 minutes. Add the minced hot pepper a little at a time to taste. Pour in the fish stock and fresh herb sachet and return to a fast simmer over high heat. Add the seared fish, potatoes, and lime peel to the pot and immediately turn the heat down to medium-low. Cook covered for 20 to 25 minutes, until the potatoes are tender but the fish is still whole.

Discard the herb sachet and lime peel and garnish with fresh parsley. Serve each bowl with a piece of fish and sprinkle with additional lime juice to taste.

Okra Stew with Plantain Dumplings

QUIMBOMBÓ CON BOLITAS DE PLÁTANO

SERVES 4 TO 6

Quimbombó *can refer to both the shooting star okra pods and the prepared stews that use them as a base. I found this* Quimbombó con Bolitas de Plátano, *made with chicken and simmered with plantain dumplings, in a friend's family cookbook written by her mother, Sara Joffre González. The chicken is first poached then marinated in sour orange juice and simmered with tomato purée and white wine to cut through the mucilage released by the okra. Native to eastern Africa, okra was first brought to the Caribbean in the sixteenth century. In the Afro-Cuban religion,* quimbombó *is a particular favorite of Changó, the deity of fire and lightening— comfort food elevated to the sacred that allows a brief respite and illuminates the path ahead.*

FOR THE STOCK

1 whole bone-in, skin-on chicken breast, split

1 large yellow onion, peeled and quartered

½ bunch fresh flat-leaf parsley

2 sprigs fresh cilantro, plus more to garnish

5 large garlic cloves, peeled and lightly crushed with the back of knife, divided

1 dried bay leaf

1 teaspoon kosher salt

1 teaspoon whole black peppercorns

FOR THE MARINADE

4 large garlic cloves, peeled

1 teaspoon kosher salt

¼ teaspoon freshly ground black pepper

½ cup freshly squeezed sour orange juice or equal parts orange and lime juice

FOR THE SOUP

¼ cup extra-virgin olive oil

1 large green bell pepper, cored, seeded, and chopped

1 medium yellow onion, peeled and chopped

1 cup Tomato Purée (page 304) or canned tomato purée

½ cup dry white wine

1 pound fresh okra, rinsed well and patted dry

Plantain Dumplings (page 97)

To make the stock, place all of the ingredients for the stock in a 6-quart heavy pot with 8 cups of water. Bring to a steady simmer over medium heat, and cook uncovered for 20 to 25 minutes.

Allow the chicken to cool in the broth. When cool enough to handle, remove and shred the chicken and place in a large mixing bowl. Strain the broth and discard the solids. Set aside 6 cups of the chicken stock.

To prepare the marinade, use a mortar and pestle to mash the garlic, salt, and black pepper to form a smooth paste. Combine the garlic paste and sour orange juice in a small measuring cup or bowl. Pour the marinade over the cooked chicken and toss until well combined.

To prepare the *sofrito*, heat the oil in a large heavy pot over medium heat. Add the green peppers and onion and sauté until the onion is soft and translucent, 6 to 8 minutes. Stir in the chicken with its marinade, reserved stock, tomato purée, and wine, then bring to a steady simmer over medium heat.

Trim the ends of the okra then slice the pods into ¼-inch rounds, dropping them into the soup pot as you go. Simmer an additional 10 to 15 minutes until the okra is tender. Add the plantain dumplings and simmer until warmed through, an additional 5 minutes. Serve immediately.

PLANTAIN DUMPLINGS
MAKES 20 TO 24 DUMPLINGS

**3 yellow plantains, trimmed and cut in half
    crosswise with peels on**

Place the plantains in a heavy pot with enough cold water to cover. Bring to a rolling boil. Lower the heat to medium and simmer covered until the plantains are tender and peeking out of the peel, about 10 minutes.

Peel the plantains when they are cool enough to handle but still warm, place in a large bowl, and mash together. Scoop out one tablespoon of mashed plantains and shape into 1-inch balls. Repeat with remaining plantains. Set aside until ready to use.

IT'S NOT EASY BEING FIRST. WHEN licenses were granted for individuals to operate private restaurants out of residential kitchens in 1994, Lilliam Domínguez Palenzuela was uniquely prepared to take advantage of the opportunity. As a little girl on her grandparents' farm in Pinar del Río, she learned to cook by watching her mother and aunts make everything from scratch—from fresh cheese and butter and corn pulled directly from the stalk to grind into meal to fried *buñuelos* and fruit preserves. A fashion designer by trade, she'd been cooking for friends in her Miramar neighborhood for years when she converted the large patio of her family's home into an open-air restaurant that became known as La Cocina de Lilliam. Since then she starts every morning by personally sourcing the ingredients they'll need while her daughter Cleo starts prepping the day's menu with their small staff of mostly home cooks. At night, Lilliam joins them in the kitchen. Making it through the early days of frequent inspections and shutdowns, she kept the doors of her *paladar* open, setting a standard for many who followed.

Galician Stew

CALDO GALLEGO

SERVES 8 TO 10

Caldo Gallego, *simmered with tender white beans, smokey ham hocks, and greens, is typical of the heartier stews that came with waves of immigration from northern Spain at the turn of the twentieth century. This version is adapted from a recipe by Siomara Molina de Venet and given to me by her daughter Lucila. When I first received it, it called for a pretty large quantity of ingredients, which Lucila helped me scale down—though she admitted that her family is just as likely to double it.*

1 pound dried white beans, such as *alubia* beans (also known as cannellini or runner beans)

2 smoked ham hocks, split

¾ pound flank steak or brisket, excess fat trimmed and cut into 3 pieces

¼ pound *tocino* or slab bacon, cut into 2 pieces

4 medium red potatoes, scrubbed, peeled, and quartered

2 medium turnips, peeled and cut into 1-inch wedges

1 large yellow onion, diced

One 3-inch piece *unto* (salt pork fat)

½ pound semi-cured Spanish-style chorizos, cut into 1-inch rounds

1 bunch collard greens, rinsed, tough stems removed, and chopped

4 large garlic cloves, peeled and mashed to a paste

¼ cup extra-virgin olive oil

Kosher salt

Freshly ground black pepper

Place the dried beans in a large mixing bowl with water to cover and soak overnight, or use the fast-soaking method (see note, page 103).

Place the ham hocks, flank steak, and *tocino* in a heavy 8-quart stockpot with 8 cups of water. Bring to a boil then reduce the heat to medium and simmer, covered, until the meats are tender, 1½ to 2 hours. Check frequently and skim off any impurities that rise to the top.

Remove the meats and dice into bite-size pieces, discarding any excess fat or bones, and set aside. Pass the broth through a fine-mesh sieve and return the broth to the pot.

Add the beans, potatoes, turnips, onion, *unto*, and chorizo and bring to a boil, then lower the heat to medium and continue to simmer, covered, until the beans and vegetables are tender, about 30 minutes. Check frequently and skim off any impurities that rise to the top. Stir in the reserved meats, collard greens, garlic paste, and olive oil. Continue to simmer until the meat is warmed through and the collard greens are wilted, an additional 10 to 15 minutes. Add salt and black pepper to taste. Drizzle with additional olive oil to serve.

NOTE

If you are making the stew on the same day, the beans can be fast-soaked. Rinse the beans well, place in a large pot with water to cover by 2 inches, and bring to a fast boil for 2 minutes. Take the beans off the heat and soak uncovered for 1 hour. Proceed with the recipe as directed.

Creole Stew with Yuca Flatbread

AJIACO CRIOLLO CON CASABE

SERVES 10 TO 12

Ajiaco is the oldest-known Cuban recipe but this version comes from a very young cook. Miguel Massens is working his way through New York's fine-dining restaurants, but he's passionate about applying everything he learns to the traditional Cuban food he grew up with. Diving into research, the first version of his recipe included two pages of footnotes that began with sixteenth-century colonial documents, detoured through nineteenth-century cooking manuals, passed through the cities of Puerto Príncipe (now Camagüey), Cárdenas, and Bayamo, and ended in Miami, where his family makes ajiaco on Christmas Day. Still, when we finally got together to make the soup in my Brooklyn kitchen, he did what all ajiaco makers have done from the start—take stock of what we had on hand, add a little of everything, and make sure that each new ingredient deepened the flavors. Soon, he was no longer just telling a story but becoming very much a part of one.

FOR THE MEATS

½ pound *tasajo de res* (smoked dried beef)

2 pounds bone-in, skinless chicken thighs and drumsticks

½ pound flank steak or brisket, cut into 1-inch cubes

½ pound bone-in *aguja de cerdo* (pork collar bones), pork ribs, or ham hock

¼ pound boneless pork loin, trimmed of any excess fat and cut into 1-inch cubes

FOR THE VEGETABLES

1 pound boniato, peeled and cut into 1-inch rounds

1 pound malanga, peeled and cut into 1-inch rounds

1 pound yuca, peeled, cored, and cut into 1-inch rounds

½ pound *ñame* (or white yam), peeled and quartered

2 ears corn, shucked and cut into 2-inch rounds

2 large green plantains, peeled and cut into 1-inch rounds

2 large yellow plantains, peeled and cut into 1-inch rounds

1 pound calabaza (sold as West Indian pumpkin), peeled, seeded, and cut into 1-inch cubes

1 chayote, peeled and cut into 1-inch cubes

FOR THE *SOFRITO*

5 large garlic cloves, peeled

1 tablespoon kosher salt

1 teaspoon freshly ground black pepper

1 teaspoon ground cumin

½ cup freshly squeezed sour orange juice or lime juice

¼ cup loosely packed fresh culantro, finely chopped

¼ cup Achiote Oil (page 298)

1 medium yellow onion, minced

5 cachucha peppers (also known as *ajíes dulces*), stemmed, seeded, and diced

1 large cubanelle pepper (also known as Italian frying pepper), stemmed, seeded, and diced

1 small fresh hot pepper (habanero, Scotch bonnet, or tabasco), stemmed, seeded, and minced (optional)

Lime juice to taste

Soak the *tasajo* to remove some of the salt, changing the water twice, at least 8 hours at room temperature or overnight.

The next day, drain the *tasajo* and rinse well under cold water.

Add the chicken, flank steak, pork collar bones, and pork loin to a heavy 8-quart stockpot with 5 quarts of water, and simmer until tender, skimming off any impurities that rise to the top, about 1 additional hour.

Add the boniato, malanga, yuca, *ñame*, and corn to the pot and continue to cook covered until the root vegetables are just tender, about 20 minutes. Add the plantains, calabaza, and chayote and continue to simmer until tender, an additional 10 to 15 minutes. Replenish the water if needed. Allow the stew to cook at lowest setting until the meat falls from the bone and shreds easily, 30 to 45 minutes.

In the meantime, prepare the *sofrito*. Using a mortar and pestle, mash the garlic, salt, black pepper, and cumin to form a smooth paste. Stir in the sour orange juice and culantro and set aside.

Heat the achiote oil in a10-inch skillet over medium heat. Add the onion and cachucha peppers and sauté until the onion is translucent, 6 to 8 minutes. Add the garlic mixture and combine with 1 cup of broth and 1 cup of root vegetables taken from the stew. Mash the vegetables into the *sofrito* and simmer until well blended, about 5 minutes. If using, add the minced hot pepper to taste. Add the entire *sofrito* to the stew and simmer an additional 10 to 15 minutes.

Adjust the seasonings to taste. Remove the chicken bones and pork bones from the stew. Ladle the stew into individual bowls and sprinkle with lime juice. Serve with warmed *Casabe* (see below) and fresh lime wedges.

NOTE

The root vegetables can be peeled, chopped, and set aside with water to cover until ready to use. The plantains can be peeled in advance and placed in a large mixing bowl with water to cover and 2 tablespoons of lime juice so they do not discolor.

CASABE | YUCA FLATBREAD

MAKES 6 LARGE FLATBREADS

Known as the "bread of the Indians," casabe is a flatbread made with shredded yuca that has been drained, dried, and lightly toasted to attain a crackerlike texture. It can be drizzled with olive oil and served with sea salt. This recipe is inspired by chef and culinary historian Maricel E. Presilla, who traveled as far as the Orinoco Basin to understand this pre-Columbian practice, which she crystallized into a few elegant steps that could be achieved simply at home.

4 pounds fresh yuca, peeled and cut into 1-inch rounds (see page 312)

2 teaspoons sea salt
Olive oil

Using a food processor, grate the yuca on the finest setting to produce a textured meal. Drain off the excess water and discard the liquid. Working in batches, wrap a small amount of yuca in a tightly woven cheesecloth and wring it out to extract as much of the liquid as possible. Repeat with the remaining yuca.

Pass the dried yuca through a coarse-mesh strainer to break up any lumps and discard the hard pieces. It will produce a couscous-like flour (about 6 cups). Stir in the salt and set aside until ready to use.

Warm a 10-inch cast-iron skillet over a medium heat until hot. Spread 1 cup of the dried pulp on the pan then press it down with a metal spatula to create a single layer. Toast until it moves in a single mass and takes on a light golden color, 2 to 3 minutes. Flip and repeat on the other side. Repeat with the remaining yuca meal. Enjoy with olive oil to taste, and a sprinkle of sea salt.

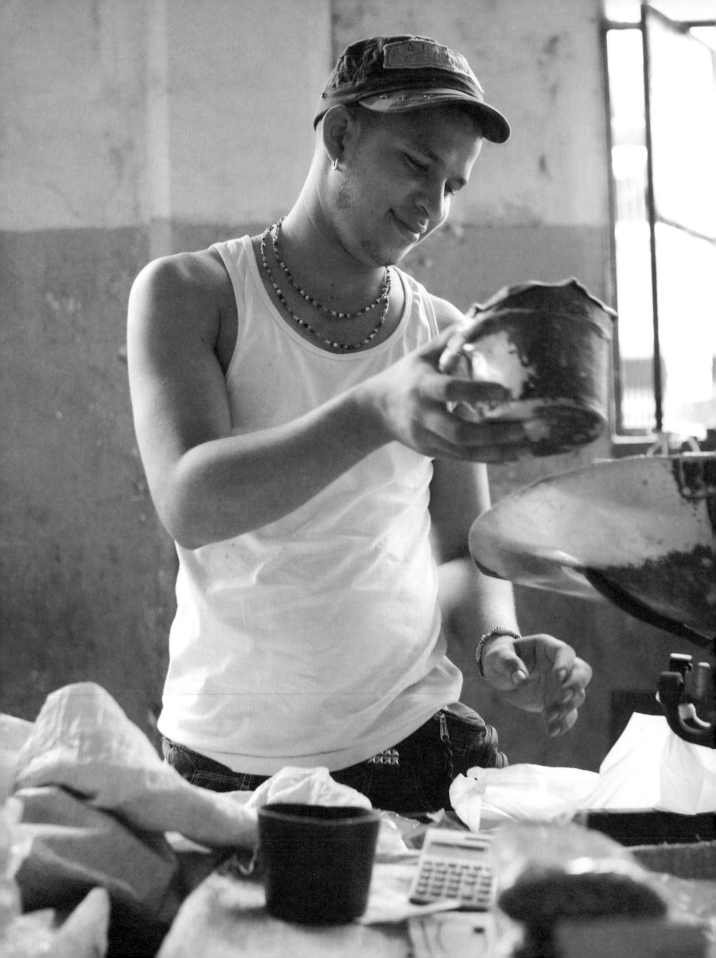

BEANS, RICE, and EGGS

Any conversation about Cuban food inevitably starts with beans. Indigenous to the island, black beans were an essential part of the pre-Columbian diet—an inky line that ties us together. In the eastern provinces, it's all about red beans—both the creamy, tender kidney beans used for a *potaje de frijoles colorados* and small red beans cooked with rice to make Oriente's famed *Congrí.* Not to be left behind, saffron-flavored *arroz con pollo* and black rice and squid swimming in sauce draw crowds while white rice anchors every meal.

POTAJE DE FRIJOLES NEGROS | *black bean pottage* . . . 113

POTAJE DE FRIJOLES COLORADOS | *red bean pottage* . . . 116

POTAJE DE GARBANZOS | *chickpea stew* . . . 119

ARROZ BLANCO | *white rice* . . . 121

CONGRÍ ORIENTAL | *eastern-style red beans and rice* . . . 125

ARROZ CON POLLO | *chicken and rice* . . . 126

ARROZ CON POLLO A LA CHORRERA |
drenched chicken and rice . . . 128

ARROZ NEGRO CON CALAMARES | *black rice with squid* . . . 132

TORTILLA ESPAÑOLA | *spanish-style tortilla* . . . 133

TORTILLA DE PLÁTANOS MADUROS |
fried ripe plantain omelet . . . 135

HUEVOS A LA MALAGUEÑA | *málaga-style eggs* . . . 136

HUEVOS EN ACEMITAS | *baked eggs in rolls* . . . 137

Black Bean Pottage

POTAJE DE FRIJOLES NEGROS

SERVES 6 TO 8

On weekends, my grandparents would spend the day preparing a large meal for us that would typically include frijoles negros *though I never ate them. I'd know lunch was almost ready when I heard my grandfather frying the egg that would go on my white rice instead of the delicious beans on everybody else's plate. My Abuelo Peláez was my favorite and I was his, so I loved the exception he made for me. It wasn't until I visited family in Spain that I gave* frijoles *a chance when they were made in my honor with the understanding that Cubans could "not live without their black beans and rice." Trying them out of politeness, I realized what a terrible mistake I'd made. By that time, my grandfather was well into his nineties and it had been a couple of years since he could manage batches of* frijoles negros. *Fortunately, it was one of the few recipes he'd written down. Using my family as Proustian proxies, I've spent many afternoons since trying to get his beans exactly the way others remember them and making up for lost time.*

FOR THE BEANS

1 pound dried black beans, rinsed well

1 large green bell pepper, stemmed, seeded, and diced

½ large white onion, diced

4 large garlic cloves, peeled and lightly crushed with the back of a knife

1 tablespoon extra-virgin olive oil

1 dried bay leaf

FOR THE *SOFRITO*

¼ cup extra-virgin olive oil

1 large green bell pepper, stemmed, seeded, and diced

½ large white onion, diced

3 large garlic cloves, peeled and finely minced

2 teaspoons kosher salt

1 teaspoon freshly ground black pepper

½ teaspoon dried oregano

½ teaspoon ground cumin

½ cup dry white wine

¼ cup green olives stuffed with pimientos, thinly sliced

1 dried bay leaf

1 to 2 tablespoons sherry vinegar

Kosher salt

Freshly ground black pepper

1 teaspoon sugar (optional)

Soak the beans overnight in a 6-quart heavy pot with 10 cups of water.

Add the next five ingredients to the beans and bring to a boil in the same soaking water. Lower the heat to medium and simmer the beans until just tender, checking regularly and skimming the foam that forms on the top, 45 to 60 minutes.

In the meantime, prepare the *sofrito*. Warm the olive oil in a 10-inch skillet over medium heat. Add the green pepper, onion, and garlic and sauté until the onion is soft and translucent, 6 to 8 minutes. Add the salt, black pepper, oregano, and cumin and cook an additional 2 minutes.

Add the *sofrito* to the pot with the beans. Stir in the wine, olives, and bay leaf. Bring the beans to a fast simmer over medium heat. Reduce the heat to medium-low and cook, covered, for 45 minutes to 1 hour. Stir frequently, until the broth has thickened and the beans are completely cooked through. Add the vinegar, salt, and black pepper to taste. Remove the beans from the heat and add the sugar if using.

Variations

For a thicker, meatier pottage, heat the oil to make the *sofrito*, then brown a ½ pound of Spanish-style chorizo, *tocino*, or slab bacon before adding the rest of the ingredients for the *sofrito*. Mash one cup of the simmered beans into the *sofrito* until well blended before adding the mixture back to the pot. Proceed with the recipe as directed.

MOROS Y CRISTIANOS

Simmer the beans, green pepper, onion, crushed garlic, olive oil, and bay leaf until just tender, about 1 hour. Drain the beans and reserve 3 cups of the cooking water. Prepare the *sofrito* as directed. Combine the beans, cooking water, and sofrito in the pot and bring to a simmer over medium heat. Add 2 cups of extra-long white rice or converted rice. Return to a simmer then turn down to the lowest possible setting and cook covered until the liquid is absorbed and the rice is tender, 20 to 30 minutes. Remove from the heat and allow the rice and beans to rest, covered, 15 minutes before serving.

FRIJOLES DORMIDOS

Soak and simmer the beans as directed. Add the *sofrito* and continue to simmer until thickened then remove from the heat before adding the final seasonings. Cool to room temperature and refrigerate, covered, overnight. The following day, warm the beans over low heat then add the vinegar, salt, black pepper, and sugar as directed.

NOTE

If the beans get away from you either by overcooking or oversalting, add more water and return to a simmer over low heat.

Red Bean Pottage

POTAJE DE FRIJOLES COLORADOS

SERVES 6 TO 8

When Nereida Pardo agreed to show me how to make Harina Dulce con Coco y Guayaba *(page 256), I was only expecting dessert but got much more, including a recipe for* Potaje de Frijoles Colorados, *which she makes with slices of calabaza and just-ripe yellow plantains.*

1 pound dried red kidney beans, rinsed well and picked through

FOR THE *SOFRITO*

1 medium yellow onion, quartered

1 large cubanelle pepper (also known as Italian frying pepper), stemmed, seeded, and quartered

5 small cachucha peppers (also known as *ajíes dulces*) stemmed, seeded, and quartered (about a ¼ cup)

4 large garlic cloves, peeled

1 tablespoon kosher salt

½ teaspoon dried oregano

¼ teaspoon ground cumin

¼ teaspoon freshly ground black pepper

¼ pound *tocino* or slab bacon, cut into ½-inch chunks

2 tablespoons Achiote Oil, (page 298)

1 cup Tomato Purée (page 304), or canned tomato purée

½ cup dry white wine

¼ cup green olives, pitted and sliced

¼ cup fresh culantro, finely chopped

1 dried bay leaf

2 large yellow plantains, cut into 1-inch chunks

1 pound calabaza (also known as West Indian Pumpkin), sliced into 2-inch wedges

1 to 2 tablespoons sherry vinegar

Soak the beans overnight in a 6-quart heavy pot with 8 cups of water.

Bring the beans to a boil in the same soaking water. Lower the heat to medium and simmer until just tender, skimming the foam that forms on the top, 45 to 60 minutes.

Combine the onion, cubanelle pepper, and cachucha peppers in a food processor and pulse until it forms a textured purée. Using a mortar and pestle, mash the garlic, salt, oregano, cumin, and black pepper to form a smooth paste.

Prepare the *sofrito*. Brown the *tocino* or bacon in a heavy skillet over medium heat until it has rendered its fat, then set aside. Replenish the skillet with achiote oil. Add the pepper purée and simmer, about 3 to 5 minutes. Add the garlic paste and sauté 5 minutes.

Add the *sofrito* to the pot with the beans. Stir in the tomato purée, wine, olives, culantro, and bay leaf and bring to a fast simmer over medium heat. Add the plantains and calabaza to the pot. Reduce the heat to medium-low and simmer, covered, stirring frequently, until the broth is slightly thickened and the vegetables are cooked through, 20 to 30 minutes. Add the reserved *tocino* and sherry vinegar and adjust the seasonings to taste.

POTAJE DE GARBANZOS

I learned how to appreciate Potaje de Garbanzos *on my first trip to Havana when I tried Nena Rodríguez's garbanzo stew. Made with smoky cuts of ham, spicy chorizo, and pillowy malanga, I loved how the rich broth wrapped itself around the chickpeas. On my second trip, her family taught me how she did it.*

FOR THE BEANS

1 pound dried chickpeas, rinsed well

1 pound bone-in cooking ham or ham hock

FOR THE *SOFRITO*

¼ cup extra-virgin olive oil

½ pound semi-cured Spanish chorizo, casings removed and sliced into ¼-inch rounds

1 medium yellow onion, diced

4 large garlic cloves, peeled and diced

2 teaspoons kosher salt

½ teaspoon freshly ground black pepper

1 cup Tomato Purée (page 304), for canned tomato purée

¼ cup dry white wine

1 teaspoon *pimentón* (Spanish-smoked paprika)

1 dried bay leaf

1 pound small red baby potatoes, quartered

½ pound white malanga, peeled and cut into 1-inch cubes

1 large red bell pepper

Place the chickpeas in a large mixing bowl in plentiful water to cover overnight, 8 to 10 hours. Drain the chickpeas and rinse well.

Combine the chickpeas and ham in a 6-quart heavy pot with 8 cups of fresh water. Bring to a boil then lower the heat to medium and simmer the beans until just tender, checking regularly and skimming the foam that forms on the top, 30 to 45 minutes. Remove the ham, debone, trim any excess fat, and cut it into 1-inch cubes and set aside.

In the meantime, prepare the *sofrito*. Heat the oil in a 10-inch skillet over medium heat. Add the chorizo and cubed ham and cook until lightly browned, 2 to 3 minutes. Add the onion, garlic, salt, and black pepper and sauté until the onion is soft and translucent, about 5 minutes.

Add the *sofrito* to the pot with the beans. Stir in the tomato purée, wine, *pimentón*, and bay leaf and simmer an additional 5 minutes. Add the potatoes and malanga, return to a simmer, and cook, covered, until the vegetables are tender, 20 to 25 minutes. Adjust the seasonings to taste.

In the meantime, roast the red pepper. Preheat the broiler. Place the red pepper on a baking sheet lined with aluminum foil and set it directly under the broiler, turning it every couple of minutes until it is charred and puckered on every side, 3 to 5 minutes. Remove the red pepper and wrap it in the aluminum foil or transfer to a plastic bag for a few minutes to "sweat." When cool enough to handle, remove the red pepper and peel off the skin. Slice the red pepper into long strips.

Add the sliced red pepper to the beans and serve as a soup or allow to cook a little longer, uncovered, for a thicker stew, about 15 minutes.

Variation: ARROZ CON GARBANZOS | RICE WITH CHICKPEAS

Simmer the beans with the ham until completely cooked through, 45 to 60 minutes. Drain the beans and reserve 3 cups of the cooking water. Prepare the *sofrito* as directed. Combine the beans, cooking water, and *sofrito* in the pot and bring to a hard simmer over medium heat. Stir in the tomato purée, wine, and bay leaf and simmer an additional 5 minutes. Omit the potatoes and malanga and add 2 cups of extra-long white rice or converted rice instead. Return to a simmer then turn down the heat to the lowest possible setting and cook, covered, until the liquid is absorbed and the rice is tender, 20 to 30 minutes. Remove from the heat and allow the rice and beans to rest, covered, 15 minutes before serving. Garnish with the roasted red pepper.

Variation: GARBANZOS FRITOS

Reduce the amount of chickpeas used to a ½ pound. Soak overnight with water to cover then drain and rinse well. Simmer the chickpeas with the ham in a heavy pot with 4 cups of fresh water until completely cooked through, 45 to 60 minutes. Drain the beans and reserve 1 cup of the cooking water. Prepare the *sofrito* as directed in a deep, heavy skillet. Stir in the roasted pepper followed by the tomato purée, wine, *pimentón*, and bay leaf and simmer an additional 5 minutes. Add the beans and cooking water to the skillet and bring to a simmer. Omit the potatoes and malanga. Keep at a steady simmer over medium heat, stirring constantly, until the liquid is largely absorbed, 15 to 20 minutes. Serve as a side dish or appetizer.

ARROZ BLANCO

SERVES 8

Brought to the table with an order of black beans in perfectly molded rounds, served in heavy chafing dishes on buffet tables, or ladled out of giant cookers from the kitchen counter, Arroz Blanco *is a blank canvas for everything from* Fricasés de Pollo *(page 150), braised dishes like* Rabo Alcaparrado *(page 166), and* Vaca Frita *(page 158).*

2 tablespoons extra-virgin olive oil

3 large garlic cloves, peeled and lightly crushed with the back of a knife

3 cups hot water

1 tablespoon kosher salt

1 dried bay leaf

2 cups long-grain white rice (see note)

Heat the oil over medium heat in a 4-quart pot with a tight-fitting lid. Add the mashed garlic cloves and sauté until lightly golden on all sides, 1 to 2 minutes. Remove the garlic cloves from the oil and discard.

Remove the pot from the heat and pour in the water. It will bubble up and sputter so this should be done carefully. Add the salt and bay leaf and bring to a fast simmer over medium-high heat. Add the rice and return to a simmer. Turn the heat down to the lowest possible setting and cook, covered, until the liquid is absorbed and the rice is tender, 25 to 30 minutes. Remove from the heat and let stand, covered, about 10 minutes. Fluff with a fork and serve.

NOTE

Rinsing rice washes away the excess starch that makes the rice clump together (good) as well as the nutrients added to replace what was stripped away during processing (not so good). Either option works well with this recipe and is a matter of personal preference.

STANDING STEADY ALONGSIDE A GIANT
antique stove and surrounded by the floor-
to-ceiling windows in our family kitchen
in La Víbora, Nena Rodríguez appeared
small but loomed large. On my first trip to
Cuba, I'd get back from a morning spent
in the city and make a direct line to Nena
who'd show me whatever kitchen miracle
she'd managed that day. Returning to
Havana years later, my first visit was to
Gertrudis and Dulce, the sisters Nena had
left behind. They offered to show me some
of the recipes I remembered from Nena
and we spent several afternoons cooking
together in their Habana Vieja apartment—frying *croquetas*, roasting chicken,
poaching guava shells, and making garbanzos. Nena wasn't where I'd hoped to
see her again, but she was everywhere.

CONGRÍ ORIENTAL

SERVES 6 TO 8

The word congrí is often used to describe either black or red beans cooked with rice. When Rosa Sabater shared her own version of Congrí Oriental *with me, she was quick to point out that true congrí is made only with the red beans they favor in the eastern provinces where she was raised. Their proximity to Haiti supports her case since the name comes from the Haitian* kongo *(beans) and* ri *(rice), though the technique itself is a legacy of West African cooks. What everyone can agree on is that the rice and beans should always be cooked together in a long, slow simmer.*

FOR THE BEANS

¾ pound small red beans, well-rinsed

FOR THE *SOFRITO*

¼ pound *tocino* or slab bacon, cut into 1-inch pieces

½ pound boneless pork shoulder, cut into 1-inch chunks

1 to 2 tablespoons extra-virgin olive oil

1 large yellow onion, diced

1 large green bell pepper, stemmed, cored, seeded, and diced

4 large garlic cloves, peeled

1 tablespoon kosher salt

½ teaspoon freshly ground black pepper

½ teaspoon dried oregano

¼ teaspoon ground cumin

¼ cup dry white wine

1 dried bay leaf

2 cups long-grain or converted white rice

Soak the beans overnight in a 6-quart heavy pot with 8 cups of water. Bring to a boil in the same soaking water. Lower the heat to medium and simmer the beans until just tender, checking regularly and skimming the foam that forms on the top, 45 to 60 minutes. Drain and reserve 3 cups of the cooking water.

While the beans simmer, prepare the *sofrito*. Brown the *tocino* in a 10-inch skillet over medium-high heat until it has rendered its fat. Remove the *tocino* and set aside. Add the pork chunks to the rendered fat, turning them until they are browned on all sides, 3 to 5 minutes. Replenish with additional olive oil as needed.

Add the onion and green pepper and sauté over medium heat until the onion is soft and translucent, 6 to 8 minutes. Using a mortar and pestle, mash the garlic, salt, black pepper, oregano, and cumin to form a smooth paste. Add the garlic paste to the skillet and sauté an additional 5 minutes.

Return the beans, cooking water, and prepared sofrito to the pot. Stir in the wine and bay leaf and bring to a simmer over medium heat. Adjust the seasonings to taste. Stir in the rice and return to a fast simmer. Turn down the heat to the lowest possible setting and cook, covered, until the liquid is absorbed and the rice is tender, 20 to 30 minutes. Garnish with reserved *tocino* and serve.

Chicken and Rice

ARROZ CON POLLO

SERVES 10

In the 1950s, when poultry was more expensive than either fish or beef, Arroz con Pollo *was the preferred dish for special occasions and Sunday family gatherings. It's a one-pot meal that's still perfect for feeding a crowd. Carmen Calzada shared her family's recipe with me.*

FOR THE CHICKEN

½ cup extra-virgin olive oil

1 medium green bell pepper, stemmed, cored, seeded, and cut in rounds

3 pounds bone-in, skin-on chicken thighs and drumsticks

FOR THE RICE

1 cup dry white wine

4 cups water

One 12-ounce bottle of pilsner-style beer, divided

½ pound asparagus, rinsed and trimmed

1 medium yellow onion, grated

1 cup jarred pimientos, drained and sliced

1 cup *petit pois* or English peas, fresh or frozen

¼ cup tomato paste

3 large garlic cloves, peeled and mashed to a paste

1 tablespoon kosher salt

1 cube chicken bouillon

¾ teaspoon freshly ground achiote seeds or *Bijol* seasoning

½ teaspoon dried oregano

½ teaspoon freshly ground nutmeg

3½ cups Valencia or similar short-grain rice, rinsed

Preheat the oven to 325°F.

Heat the olive oil over medium-high heat in an ovenproof, 6-quart heavy pot or Dutch oven until hot but not smoking. Add the green pepper to the oil. Working in batches, brown the chicken on both sides, 2 to 3 minutes per side. Set aside the browned chicken and repeat with remaining pieces. Remove the green pepper and discard.

To deglaze the pot, add the wine and bring to a simmer, scraping up the browned bits. Return the browned chicken to the pot. Add the remaining ingredients except for the rice, and half the beer and part of the pimientos to add at the end. Bring to a simmer.

Stir in the rice and simmer over medium-high heat for 10 minutes. Remove the pot from direct heat, cover with a tight-fitting lid, and set in the preheated oven, and bake until the rice is tender but still moist, about 20 minutes.

Remove from the oven and immediately pour in the remaining beer. Garnish with the reserved pimientos.

ARROZ CON POLLO A LA CHORRERA

SERVES 8

Many people believe Arroz con Pollo a la Chorrera *gets its name from the beer that gives the rice a risotto-like consistency. It actually comes from a dish made famous in the nineteenth century at La Chorrera del Vedado by hotel chef Alfred Petit. The hotel itself was named after the Torreón de la Chorrera, a fortress at the mouth of the Almendares River that cuts through Havana, so maybe it comes down to a long pour after all. I learned to make this version with my aunt Cristina Oyarzun, who shreds the chicken before returning it to the pot. At this point it can be chilled overnight so the flavors develop, breaking up the work, and making it a great do-ahead dinner.*

FOR THE MARINADE

3 large garlic cloves, peeled

1 tablespoon kosher salt

¼ teaspoon freshly ground black pepper

1 cup freshly squeezed sour orange juice, or equal parts orange and lime juice

3 pounds bone-in, skinless chicken thighs and drumsticks

FOR THE *SOFRITO*

¼ cup extra-virgin olive oil, plus more if needed

1 medium yellow onion, diced

1 medium green bell pepper, stemmed, cored, seeded, and diced

3 large garlic cloves, peeled and diced

FOR THE RICE

1 cup dry white wine

1½ cups Tomato Purée (page 304), or canned tomato purée

1 cup jarred pimientos, drained and sliced

2 dried bay leaves

5 cups Chicken Stock (page 306), or store-bought chicken stock

1 teaspoon dried oregano

½ teaspoon ground cumin

½ teaspoon saffron threads

3 cups Valencia or similar short-grain rice, rinsed

One 12-ounce bottle of pilsner-style beer

1 cup marinated artichokes, drained and chopped

½ to 1 cup *petit pois* or English peas, fresh, or thawed if frozen

Kosher salt

Freshly ground black pepper

Additional pimientos

To prepare the marinade, use a mortar and pestle to mash together three garlic cloves, salt, and black pepper to form a smooth paste. Stir in the sour orange juice to combine. Place the chicken pieces in a large mixing bowl and pour the marinade over the chicken. Cover the bowl with plastic wrap and allow the chicken to marinate in the refrigerator at least 2 hours or overnight.

Remove the chicken from the marinade, drain, and pat dry. Reserve the marinade for later use. Heat the olive oil in a 6-quart heavy pot or Dutch oven over medium-high heat until hot but not smoking. Working in batches, brown the chicken pieces on both sides, 2 to 3 minutes per side. Replenish with additional olive oil as needed. Remove the chicken pieces and set aside.

Add the onion, green pepper, and three diced garlic cloves to the same pot used for browning the chicken. Sauté over medium heat until the onion is soft and translucent, 6 to 8 minutes. To deglaze the pot, add the wine and bring to a simmer, scraping up the browned bits. Add the reserved marinade, tomato purée, pimientos, and bay leaves. Return the browned chicken to the pot and simmer until cooked through, about 30 minutes.

Carefully lift the chicken pieces out of the pot and transfer to a cutting board. When cool enough to handle, shred the chicken. Return the shredded chicken to the pot. Stir in chicken stock, oregano, cumin, and saffron then return to a high simmer (see note).

Stir in the rice and return to a simmer. Turn down the heat to the lowest possible setting and cook, covered, until the liquid is absorbed and the rice is tender, 25 to 30 minutes.

Add the artichokes and peas to the pot. Pour in the beer and continue to cook an additional 5 minutes. Adjust the seasonings to taste. Garnish with additional pimientos.

NOTE

At this point, the stew can be covered and refrigerated overnight. When ready to serve, return the pot to a simmer over medium heat, add the rice, and proceed with the recipe as directed.

Black Rice with Squid

ARROZ NEGRO CON CALAMARES

SERVES 6

Like many regional Spanish dishes, Arroz Negro con Calamares *was brought by immigrants from Catalunya but became part of the larger Creole cuisine once it landed in Cuba. I was given this recipe by my friend Nathalie Marcos. Always looking for a reason to have a dinner party, her small Manhattan kitchen is stockpiled with a market's worth of bouillon cubes and spices, bottles of* vino seco, *tins of* calamares, *and bags of Valencia rice she brings back from Miami to keep her favorite ingredients from home at hand.*

¼ cup extra-virgin olive oil

6 large garlic cloves

1 teaspoon sea salt

½ teaspoon freshly ground black pepper

1 medium yellow onion, diced

1 pound fresh squid, cleaned, rinsed, and sliced into rings ½ inch thick

1 cup jarred pimientos, drained and diced, plus more for garnish

1 teaspoon smoked *pimentón* (Spanish-style paprika)

1 teaspoon dried oregano

2 cups water

2 cups Fish Stock (page 307), or store-bought fish stock

1 cup dry white wine

1 to 2 teaspoons squid ink

3 cups Valencia rice or similar short-grain rice

Make the *sofrito.* Using a mortar and pestle, mash the garlic, salt, and black pepper to form a smooth paste. Heat the oil in a 5- to 6-quart heavy pot. Add the onion and garlic paste and sauté 6 to 8 minutes. Add the squid and red peppers and cook an additional 5 minutes. Add the *pimentón* and oregano. Stir in the water, fish stock, wine, and squid ink to taste and bring to a simmer.

Stir in the rice and return to a fast simmer. Turn the heat down to the lowest possible setting and cook, covered, until the rice is tender, 20 to 25 minutes. The liquid should be partly absorbed but the rice should still be moist. Adjust the seasonings to taste. Garnish with additional pimientos.

Spanish-style Tortilla
TORTILLA ESPAÑOLA
SERVES 6

Tortilla Española is the first dish I made for my grandparents, and I still remember my relief when my grandfather Ramón announced I had found el punto de la papa—*the point where the potatoes are cooked just enough to easily split in half without falling apart. The flip is the most nerve-wrecking part and I'm superstitious about anyone else being in the kitchen when I do it. This also buys time in case you need to repair any damage.*

1 cup olive oil

4 medium red potatoes (about
   1½ pounds), peeled and cut into
   slices ¼-inch thick

1 medium yellow onion, chopped

8 extra-large eggs

1 teaspoon kosher salt

¼ teaspoon freshly ground black pepper

Heat the oil over medium heat in a deep 10-inch skillet. Add the potatoes and onion to the skillet. Turn the potatoes often so that they cook evenly and do not brown. Sauté until the potatoes are just tender and break apart with slight pressure, about 20 minutes.

Beat the eggs with the salt and black pepper in a mixing bowl. Remove the potatoes and onion from the skillet with a slotted spoon and add to the beaten eggs. Adjust the salt to taste. Strain the oil into a measuring cup or bowl and wipe out the skillet to remove any browned pieces before adding the eggs so the omelet slides out easily when flipped.

Heat 1 tablespoon of the strained oil in the skillet over medium heat until hot but not smoking. Add the egg mixture to the skillet and cook until the eggs begin to set and the underside is lightly browned.

Remove the skillet from the heat and cover with a large plate. Holding the plate down firmly, quickly turn over the skillet so that the tortilla slides out onto the plate. Return the skillet to medium heat and add additional oil if needed. Slide tortilla back into the skillet and cook on the other side, an additional 5 to 7 minutes or until it reaches the desired degree of doneness.

Flip the tortilla one more time onto a serving plate. Serve at room temperature, sliced into wedges or cut into squares.

Variation: TORTILLA DE PAPAS Y CHORIZO

Heat the 1 tablespoon of oil in the skillet and brown ½ pound Spanish-style semi-cured chorizo, casing removed and cut into ¼-inch rounds. Remove from the skillet and add the rest of the oil. Add 1 diced green bell pepper, to the potatoes and onion and simmer together. Combine the eggs, chorizo, and potato mixture. Proceed as directed.

Fried Ripe Plantain Omelet

TORTILLA DE PLÁTANOS MADUROS

SERVES 6

Fried plantains make this a very Creole rendition of the classic Spanish omelet.

½ cup olive oil

2 garlic cloves, peeled and lightly crushed
    with the back of a knife

3 large ripe plantains, peeled and cut into
    diagonal slices 1-inch long

8 extra-large eggs

1 teaspoon kosher salt

½ teaspoon freshly ground black pepper

Heat the oil over medium heat in a 10-inch skillet. Add the mashed garlic and cook until golden on all sides, 1 to 2 minutes. Remove the garlic from the oil and discard. Add the plantains and cook until they are a deep amber with black edges. Remove the plantains from the skillet and drain on a plate lined with paper towels. Set aside.

Beat together the eggs, salt, and pepper in a separate bowl. Stir in the fried plantains. Pour out all but about 1 tablespoon of oil from the skillet and return to medium heat. Add the egg mixture to the skillet and cook until the eggs begin to set and the underside is lightly browned.

Remove the skillet from the heat and cover with a large plate. Holding the plate down firmly, quickly turn over the skillet so that the tortilla slides out onto the plate. Return the skillet to medium heat and add additional oil if needed. Slide the tortilla back onto the skillet and cook on the other side an additional 3 to 5 minutes or until it reaches the desired degree of doneness.

Flip the tortilla one more time onto a serving plate. Serve at room temperature either sliced into wedges for individual portions or cut into squares as an appetizer.

Málaga-style Eggs

HUEVOS A LA MALAGUEÑA

SERVES 6

In this traditional Cuban dish with Spanish inspiration, Camarones Enchilados *(page 189) are transformed into* Huevos a la Malagueña—*spicy shrimp blended with ham and asparagus then topped with an egg and baked.*

2 cups Camarones Enchilados (page 189)

½ pound asparagus, trimmed and diced

½ pound cured Spanish-style chorizo, casings removed and cubed into ¼-inch pieces

6 large eggs

Fresh flat-leaf parsley, leaves and tender stems, finely chopped

Sea salt

Freshly ground black pepper

Tabasco sauce

SPECIAL EQUIPMENT:

Six 10-ounce ceramic ramekins or small baking dishes

Preheat the oven to 400°F. Line a baking sheet with parchment paper

Place ⅓ cup of the prepared *Camarones Enchilados* in each ramekin. Distribute the chorizo and asparagus evenly among the ramekins. Crack an egg into a small bowl or cup and gently drop into each ramekin. Place the ramekins on the baking sheet and put in the oven and bake until the whites are set, 15 to 20 minutes. Garnish with parsley and sprinkle with sea salt, black pepper, and Tabasco sauce to taste.

HUEVOS EN ACEMITAS

SERVES 6

The best recipe is always the one you can't quite remember. For months, I searched for these Huevos en Acemitas—*eggs baked with béchamel sauce, ham, and peas inside sweet rolls. This was a childhood favorite of my mother's, so she suggested I consult* el libro de Tita Marta. *Newly married in 1949, my great-aunt Marta Fontanills Lizama started copying down her favorite recipes in an enormous green ledger. Fortunately, she kept good accounts and took down everyone else's, too. There were even a few my mother had given her when she was a little girl, which doesn't surprise me, because Tita Marta always took children very seriously.*

FOR THE BÉCHAMEL SAUCE

2 tablespoons unsalted butter

1½ tablespoons unbleached all-purpose flour

1 cup whole milk

1 teaspoon kosher salt

¼ teaspoon freshly ground white pepper

1 pinch freshly ground nutmeg

6 small Pan de Media Noche (page 300) rolls or similar brioche-style rolls

¼ pound sweet-cured ham, trimmed and cubed

¼ cup fresh *petit pois* or English peas, fresh or frozen

2 large plum tomatoes, diced

6 large eggs

Kosher salt

Freshly ground white pepper to taste

Preheat the oven to 375°F. Line a baking sheet with parchment paper.

Melt the butter in a heavy saucepan over medium-low heat. Add the flour and cook, stirring constantly until well blended but not browned, about 2 minutes. Gradually pour in the milk and stir until the sauce has thickened and the whisk leaves trace marks on the surface, 5 additional minutes. Stir in the salt, white pepper, and nutmeg to taste and set aside to cool.

Cut out a round circle from the top of each roll, remove the circle and set aside. Scoop out the bread inside the roll to create a round opening for the filling, allowing a ½-inch border. Lightly butter the circles or tops and set aside.

Arrange the rolls and tops on the prepared baking sheet. Drop 2 tablespoons of béchamel sauce in each roll, followed by the cubed ham, peas, and tomatoes. Crack an egg into a small bowl or cup and gently drop into each roll to cover the fillings. Place in the oven and bake until the egg whites are set, 15 to 20 minutes. Season with salt and white pepper to taste and serve the filled rolls with their tops for dipping.

CHICKEN, BEEF, and PORK

Lechón asado—*said quickly so it's one word followed by a pause and a sigh*—is by far the most common response given by Cubans when asked for their favorite dish to both prepare and eat. But that's only part of the story. Chicken stews in the form of sweet-and-sour *fricasés* are family favorites that work their way into pies and empanadas. Thinly pounded *palomilla* steaks marinated in lime juice are seared in a skillet and drowned in onions. Inexpensive cuts such as oxtail and goat are cooked in a peppery, tomato-based sofrito then braised to the fainting point before being ladled over white rice and served with fried ripe plantains. It's the *sabor familiar* of everyone preparing these dishes together that people enjoy the most. When there's time, they adhere to the traditional methods—the requisite slow simmer becoming an easy excuse to gather around the stove. When there's not enough time, there's always the pressure cooker—the *cha-cha-cha* of the round metal gauge keeping time and providing a sound track for home chefs at work, ready to welcome anyone who might join them.

PASTEL DE POLLO | *chicken pie* . . . 143

POLLO FRITO A LA CRIOLLA | *creole fried chicken* . . . 149

FRICASÉ DE POLLO | *chicken fricassée* . . . 150

BISTEC DE PALOMILLA | *pan-fried steak* . . . 152

BOLICHE MECHADO | *stuffed pot roast* . . . 154

PICADILLO CLÁSICO | *classic beef picadillo* . . . 157

VACA FRITA | *lime-marinated crispy beef* . . . 158

CARNE CON PAPAS Y ZANAHORIAS | *beef stew with fingerling potatoes and baby heirloom carrots* . . . 161

ROPA VIEJA | *"old clothes" braised beef with peppers and onions* . . . 162

CHILINDRÓN DE CHIVO | *goat stew* . . . 164

RABO ALCAPARRADO | *oxtail in caper sauce* . . . 166

LECHÓN ASADO | *oven-roasted pork shoulder* . . . 169

MASAS DE PUERCO | *fried pork chunks* . . . 172

BUTIFARRAS | *fresh pork sausages* . . . 174

CARNE DE CERDO ADOBADO | *pork loin in adobo* . . . 178

Chicken Pie

PASTEL DE POLLO

SERVES 6

This Pastel de Pollo *filled with gently stewed shredded chicken stuffed into a barely sweet dough is a direct descendant of the famed Galician pies sold to pilgrims on the road to Santiago de Compostela. Encarnación Gómez Betancourt taught me the recipe when I visited her in Camagüey on my way to the National Shrine Basilica of Our Lady of Charity in El Cobre, so it was an unexpectedly appropriate choice.*

FOR THE PASTRY

2 cups unbleached all-purpose flour

¼ cup sugar

1 tablespoon baking powder

1 teaspoon kosher salt

½ cup whole milk at room temperature

⅓ cup canola oil

1 large egg, beaten with 1 tablespoon of water

FOR THE FILLING

1 medium yellow onion, finely chopped

1 medium green bell pepper, stemmed, cored, seeded, and finely chopped

3 large garlic cloves, peeled and diced

1 teaspoon kosher salt

¼ teaspoon freshly ground black pepper

¼ teaspoon ground cumin

¼ cup extra-virgin olive oil

1 whole bone-in, skinless chicken breast, split

1 cup diced tomatoes, canned or fresh, with their juice

¼ cup dry white wine

1 dried bay leaf

½ pound red potatoes, peeled and cubed

½ cup green olives, pitted and sliced

To prepare the pastry, sift together the dry ingredients in a large mixing bowl. Create a well in the middle of the flour and pour in the milk and oil then stir to blend. Knead by hand to form a smooth dough, 3 to 5 minutes. Shape the dough into two round discs, wrap in plastic, and refrigerate at least 1 hour or overnight.

To prepare the filling, process the onion and green peppers in a food processor to form a textured purée. Using a mortar and pestle, mash together the garlic, salt, black pepper, and cumin to form a smooth paste.

Heat the oil over medium heat in a deep 10-inch skillet. Add the onion-green pepper purée, and garlic paste and sauté until fragrant, 3 to 5 minutes. Add the chicken breast, tomatoes, wine, and bay leaf. Bring to a simmer and cook partially covered until the chicken is cooked through, 20 to 30 minutes.

Remove the chicken breast, debone, shred, and return to the skillet. Stir in the potatoes and olives. Continue to simmer, covered, until the potatoes are cooked through, an additional 10 to 15 minutes. Remove from the heat and set aside.

Preheat the oven to 425°F.

To fill the pastry, roll out the first disc on a lightly floured board to a 10-inch round, about ⅛ inch thick. Spread chicken filling on the rolled pastry, leaving ½-inch border. Brush the egg wash around the border. Refrigerate until ready to use.

Roll out the remaining dough and place on top of the filled pastry, pressing down along the border to seal. Brush the tops with beaten egg wash. Place in the preheated oven and bake until lightly golden, 20 to 25 minutes. Allow to cool then slice and serve.

I SET OUT TO FIND ENCARNACIÓN GÓMEZ
Betancourt on the borrowed memories
of her nephew Mario who'd described
the wonderful meals she'd prepare for
him. Only moments after arriving in her
kitchen, I realized they were all true. A
cook in constant motion, she quickly filled
a piecrust, rolled out a second one, and
started a savory chicken filling for a third. It
seemed like nothing was close to finished,
but we didn't wait long. With two ovens
going and several pots on the stove, she'd
give the children and grandchildren who
surrounded her silent directions that mate-
rialized in tables moved into the garden,
well-laid place settings, steaming tureens
of *sopa de frijoles*, ham steaks, platters of
pastel de pollo, and a sky-high layered cake.
For years, she'd worked in Camagüey's
Casa de Huéspedes, welcoming people
into the city, and she takes the same care
with every meal. As she explained, "Food
is sacred. Even for something as simple
as eating a fried egg, the table should be
worthy of it."

Creole Fried Chicken

POLLO FRITO A LA CRIOLLA

SERVES 6 TO 8

Steeped in a sour orange juice marinade with plenty of onions, garlic, oregano, and cumin, this chicken can be simmered on the stove top or roasted in the oven.

3 pounds bone-in, skin-on chicken thighs and drumsticks

4 large garlic cloves, peeled

1 teaspoon dried oregano

1 teaspoon ground cumin

1 teaspoon kosher salt

¼ teaspoon freshly ground black pepper

1 cup freshly squeezed sour orange juice, or equal parts lime and orange juice

1 large yellow onion, thinly sliced

¼ to ½ cup olive oil, plus more if needed

½ cup dry white wine

Place the chicken in a large mixing bowl. Using a mortar and pestle, mash the garlic, oregano, cumin, salt, and pepper to a paste. Stir in the sour orange juice. Pour the marinade over the chicken pieces, top with the sliced onions, and refrigerate, covered, for at least 3 hours or overnight.

Remove the chicken and onions from the marinade, drain, and pat dry. Reserve the marinade for later use.

Heat the olive oil in a 6-quart cast-iron or heavy-bottomed pot over medium-high heat until hot but not smoking. Working in batches, brown the chicken on both sides until the fat is rendered, 2 to 3 minutes per side. Do not overcrowd the pot. Replenish the oil as needed. Set aside the browned chicken pieces.

Pour out all but 2 tablespoons of the oil and sauté the reserved onions in the pot until soft and translucent, about 5 minutes. Stir in the reserved marinade and wine and bring to a simmer. Return the browned chicken pieces to the pot and lower the heat. Cook, partially covered, until the chicken is cooked through, 25 to 30 minutes.

Chicken Fricassée

FRICASÉ DE POLLO

SERVES 6 TO 8

This Fricasé de Pollo *comes from my aunt Natasha Oyarzun, a master of her kitchen island, who always has something on the stove, a new ingredient she wants you to try, or a twist on a classic recipe she's willing to share. Though* fricasés *came to Cuba from France by way of Haiti, the French might not recognize their white-sauce stew in this sweet-and-sour blend of citrus juices, pepper* sofrito, *briny olives, plump raisins, and balsamic vinegar. But they might enjoy it just the same.*

FOR THE MARINADE

3 garlic cloves, peeled

1 teaspoon kosher salt

1 teaspoon dried oregano

½ teaspoon ground cumin

½ teaspoon freshly ground black pepper

1 cup freshly squeezed sour orange juice, or equal parts lime and orange juice

¼ cup freshly squeezed lime juice

4 pounds bone-in, skin-on chicken thighs (about 10 to 12 pieces)

FOR THE STEW

½ cup olive oil

1 medium yellow onion, finely chopped

½ medium red bell pepper, stemmed, cored, seeded, and finely chopped

½ medium green bell pepper, stemmed, cored, seeded, and finely chopped

4 garlic cloves, peeled and diced

1 cup dry white wine

1 cup Chicken Stock (page 306), or store-bought chicken stock

1 cup tomato sauce

1 teaspoon dried oregano

½ teaspoon ground cumin

2 pounds baby red potatoes, scrubbed and quartered

¼ cup Manzanilla green olives, pitted

½ cup raisins

¼ to ½ cup balsamic vinegar

Kosher salt

Freshly ground black pepper

To prepare the marinade, use a mortar and pestle to mash the garlic, salt, oregano, and cumin to a paste. Blend in the sour orange and lime juices to combine. Place the chicken pieces in a large mixing bowl. Pour the marinade over the chicken and cover the bowl with plastic wrap. Allow the chicken to marinate in the refrigerator at least 2 hours or overnight.

Remove the chicken from the marinade, drain, and pat dry. Reserve the marinade for later use.

Heat the olive oil in a heavy 5- to 6-quart pot over medium heat until hot but not smoking. Working in batches, brown the chicken on both sides until the fat is rendered, 2 to 3 minutes per side. Remove the chicken and discard the skin. Set aside until ready to use.

Add the onion, red and green peppers, and garlic to the pot where you browned the chicken. Stir constantly over medium heat until the onion is soft and translucent, about 5 minutes. Add the wine, chicken stock, tomato sauce, and reserved marinade. Stir in the remaining oregano and cumin. Return the browned chicken to the pot and simmer until cooked through, covered, about 40 minutes.

Add the potatoes, olives, raisins, and balsamic vinegar to taste. Continue to cook, covered, until the potatoes are cooked through, an additional 15 to 20 minutes.

Pan-Fried Steak

BISTEC DE PALOMILLA

SERVES 4

Bistec de Palomilla was a favorite of my father's. Early pickups from school were an excuse to go to Leila's Restaurant in Miami where the steaks were served under a mountain of Papas Fritas a la Juliana *(page 64) and it was our secret. Made at home, they are more often* encebollado, *smothered in lightly steamed onions, sprinkled with lime juice, and garnished with fresh parsley. Either way, it's a dish I associate with stolen hours.*

1½ pounds top-round or sirloin steak, cut into 4 pieces and pounded to a ¼ inch thick

FOR THE MARINADE

4 large garlic cloves

1 teaspoon sea salt

¼ teaspoon freshly ground black pepper

¼ cup freshly squeezed lime juice, plus wedges to serve

2 tablespoons olive oil, plus more as needed

1 large yellow onion, thinly sliced

¼ cup fresh flat-leaf parsley, leaves and tender stems, finely chopped

Place the steaks in a large mixing bowl. Using a mortar and pestle, mash together the garlic, sea salt, and pepper to form a paste. Whisk in the lime juice until well blended. Pour the marinade over the steaks and refrigerate for 1 hour.

Heat the olive oil in a heavy 12-inch skillet over medium-high heat until hot but not smoking. Remove the steaks from the marinade, drain, and pat dry. Reserve the marinade. Working in batches, add the steaks to the skillet, turning them once until they are browned, about 1 to 2 minutes per side. Repeat with the remaining steaks and replenish the oil as needed.

Pour the marinade into the skillet and bring to a simmer to deglaze. Add the onion to the skillet then immediately cover and take off the heat. Keep covered until the onions are lightly steamed but still crisp, 1 to 2 minutes. Pour the onions over the steaks and sprinkle with parsley. Serve with additional lime wedges and white rice.

Variations: BISTEC EMPANIZADO | CHICKEN FRIED STEAK

Pound the steaks to a ½ inch thick then marinade the steaks as directed. Combine 1 cup cracker meal, 2 tablespoons unbleached all-purpose flour, 1 teaspoon kosher salt, and ¼ teaspoon freshly ground black pepper in a small bowl. In a separate bowl, beat together

3 extra-large eggs. Remove the steak from the marinade and pat dry. Dredge the steaks in the cracker meal, then the beaten eggs, then the cracker meal again until well coated. Heat 2 inches of peanut or canola oil in a heavy skillet over medium-high heat until hot but not smoking. Working in batches, add the coated steaks to the skillet and fry until golden brown on both sides, 3 to 4 minutes. Transfer the steaks to a plate lined with paper towels. Serve with lime wedges and white rice.

Variations: PAN CON BISTEC

Prepare the *bistec de palomilla* as directed. Slice 4 loaves of *Pan de Agua* (page 299) in half lengthwise. Layer each bottom half with the *palomilla*, end to end. Cover with steamed onions or top with shredded lettuce, sliced tomato, and shoestring fries. Cut on the diagonal and serve.

BOLICHE MECHADO

SERVES 4 TO 6

As a working mother, Carmen López Gómez says she didn't have a lot of time to spend in the kitchen, but her daughter remembers her pulling together full family meals every night in what seemed like minutes. One of her secrets was this Boliche Mechado *stuffed with chorizo. Made in advance, it can be frozen inside its braising liquid and reheated without missing a beat.*

FOR THE ROAST

4 pounds boneless beef eye of round roast

4 ounces Spanish-style cured chorizo, casings removed

8 large garlic cloves, peeled

2 teaspoons kosher salt

FOR THE *SOFRITO*

½ cup extra-virgin olive oil

1 large yellow onion, diced

1 teaspoon dried oregano

1 teaspoon kosher salt

¼ teaspoon freshly ground black pepper

1 cup water

1 cup dry red wine

½ cup freshly squeezed orange juice

½ cup pimiento-stuffed whole olives plus more to garnish

2 large bay leaves

Place the roast in a shallow baking pan. Using a sharp knife, bore a hole through the center of the roast to create a 1-inch cavity. Fill with chorizo. Using a mortar and pestle, mash together the garlic and salt to form a smooth paste. Rub the entire roast with the garlic paste until well covered. Cover in plastic wrap and refrigerate, 1 hour or preferably overnight.

Heat the olive oil in a 6-quart pressure cooker over medium-high heat until hot but not smoking. Brown the roast on all sides, 5 to 8 minutes. Add the onion, oregano, salt, and pepper and sauté until the onion is soft and translucent, 6 to 8 minutes.

Add the water, wine, orange juice, olives, and bay leaves and bring to a simmer. Seal the pressure cooker. Heat on high for 5 minutes then reduce the heat to medium and cook for 45 additional minutes. Do not remove the lid until the pressure comes down completely per manufacturer's instructions.

Transfer the roast to a cutting board and allow to rest, about 10 minutes. Carve the roast into 1-inch slices and return the slices to the pot with the liquid. Bring the remaining sauce in the pot to a hard simmer, uncovered, until reduced by half, 10 to 15 minutes. Adjust the seasonings to taste. Serve the sliced roast with the sauce.

NOTE

Prepared in advance, the *boliche* will keep well in the freezer, well-wrapped, for up to 1 month. Defrost in the refrigerator then slice and warm in its braising liquid to serve.

PICADILLO CLÁSICO

SERVES 6

Beef Picadillo *is on most families weekly rotation. I learned how to make it long distance with my grandmother Alicia on speakerphone talking me through the steps as I prepared it for my college roommates. She rarely cooked but knew how to give directions. Served over white rice with* Plátanos Maduros *(page 135) and followed by* Poached Guava Shells *(page 266), it's my favorite recipe to make for my Cuban friends who miss home and my non-Cuban friends who don't know what they're missing. Easily the most versatile recipe, it can be used as a filling for pastries, empanadas, tamales, and fritters.*

¼ cup extra-virgin olive oil

1 medium yellow onion, diced

1 large green bell pepper, stemmed, cored, seeded, and diced

3 large garlic cloves, peeled and minced

1 teaspoon kosher salt

1 teaspoon dried oregano

½ teaspoon ground cumin

¼ teaspoon freshly ground black pepper

2 tablespoons tomato paste

1 pound lean ground beef

1 cup diced tomatoes, fresh or canned, in their juice

¼ cup dry white wine

¼ cup pimiento-stuffed green olives, halved

¼ cup dark raisins

1 tablespoon capers

1 tablespoon sherry vinegar

2 tablespoons fresh flat-leaf parsley, leaves and tender stems, finely chopped

2 tablespoons fresh oregano, finely chopped

Heat the oil in a 10-inch skillet over medium heat. Add the onion, green pepper, garlic, salt, dried oregano, cumin, and black pepper and sauté until the onion is translucent, 6 to 8 minutes. Add the tomato paste and stir until well combined, an additional 2 minutes.

Raise the heat to high and brown the beef, breaking it up so there are no lumps. Stir in the tomatoes, wine, olives, raisins, and capers. Reduce the heat to low and simmer, covered, 15 to 20 minutes, stirring occasionally.

Stir in the sherry vinegar and adjust the seasonings to taste. Garnish with chopped parsley and fresh oregano.

Variation: PICADILLO A CABALLO

Similar to *fritas*, picadillo can be topped with fried eggs and potatoes to make it *a caballo*. Prepare the picadillo as directed. Peel and dice 1 pound of russet potatoes. Heat 1 tablespoon of olive oil in a separate skillet over medium-high heat. Add the potatoes to the oil and cook until lightly golden, 8 to 10 minutes. Transfer to the picadillo and top with fried eggs.

Lime-Marinated Crispy Beef

VACA FRITA

SERVES 6

For professor and chef Lourdes Castro, citrus adds a brightness to Cuban cooking that is often overlooked. In her recipe for Vaca Frita *or "fried cow," the beef is simmered until it shreds easily, then marinated in lime juice and olive oil. According to Lourdes, the key to achieving a perfectly blackened texture is to work in batches to achieve crispy—not steamed—beef.*

1½ pounds flank steak, excess fat trimmed, and cut into 4 pieces

2 medium yellow onions, one cut in half and the other thinly sliced

1 dried bay leaf

½ cup freshly squeezed lime juice

3 large garlic cloves, peeled

1½ teaspoons kosher salt, divided

3 tablespoons olive oil

½ teaspoon freshly ground black pepper

Place the beef, onion halves, and bay leaf in a deep saucepan with enough water to cover the ingredients. Bring to a boil then reduce to a simmer and cook, uncovered, for 20 minutes.

Remove the saucepan from the heat. Allow the beef to cool in the broth, so it will stay moist and juicy. Drain and save the broth for future use if desired.

When cool enough to handle, shred the beef by hand, pulling apart its fibers with your fingers.

Using a mortar and pestle, mash the garlic with ½ teaspoon of salt to form a paste. Place the shredded beef in a bowl and toss with the onion slices, lime juice, garlic paste, and olive oil until well combined. Allow to marinate for at least 30 minutes or up to a few hours.

Heat a nonstick 12-inch skillet over medium-high heat. Toss the marinated beef and season with the remaining teaspoon of salt and black pepper. Working in batches, add just enough beef to the skillet to fill it in a single layer (there is no need to add more oil as the marinade has a sufficient amount). Allow the beef to sear for 3 minutes, undisturbed, in order to achieve a crispy texture. Stir the beef and allow it to cook for another 2 minutes. Remove and repeat with the remaining beef. Serve with *Arroz Blanco* (page 121) and *Plátanos Maduros* (page 135).

NOTE

The beef can be left marinating a few hours in advance. You can also sear the beef about 1½ hours before serving and hold it in a warm 250°F oven.

Beef Stew with Fingerling Potatoes and Baby Heirloom Carrots

CARNE CON PAPAS Y ZANAHORIAS

SERVES 6 TO 8

Sonia Zaldívar shared this Carne con Papas y Zanahorias *made at Victor's Café. A comforting stew of slow-cooked beef and potatoes often made at home, it rarely appears on restaurant menus. It was a fitting recipe to include from the family-owned landmark restaurant where those distinctions never really mattered.*

3 pounds top-round beef, trimmed of any excess fat, and cut into 4-inch medallions

Kosher salt

3 large whole carrots, peeled and roughly chopped

1 large tomato, roughly chopped

1 small red bell pepper, stemmed, cored, seeded, and roughly chopped

1 small green bell pepper, stemmed, cored, seeded, and roughly chopped

1 medium yellow onion, roughly chopped

4 large garlic cloves, peeled

¼ cup extra-virgin olive oil, plus more as needed

2 cups Tomato Purée (page 304), or canned tomato purée

¼ cup light soy sauce

1 cup red wine

4 cups Beef Stock (page 306), or store-bought beef stock

1 dried bay leaf

24 small fingerling potatoes

18 baby heirloom carrots

Preheat the oven to 300°F.

Season the beef with salt and set aside. Combine the carrots, tomato, green and red peppers, onion, and garlic in a food processor and pulse to mince. Heat the oil over medium-high heat in a 6-quart ovenproof pot or Dutch oven. Working in batches, add the beef and sear on all sides until browned. Remove the beef and set aside. Repeat with the remaining beef medallions.

Add the minced vegetables to the pot and sauté over medium-high heat until the onion is soft and translucent. Add the tomato purée and soy sauce to deglaze the pot. Add the red wine and simmer until the mixture is reduced by half. Add the beef stock and bring to a boil, then lower the heat and simmer for 7 to 10 minutes. Season with salt to taste.

Add the browned beef to the pot, making sure that it is covered completely by the liquid. Cover the pan and cook in the oven for 2 hours. Add the potatoes and baby carrots to the beef and cook in the oven for 1 more hour. Remove from the oven and allow the stew to cool slightly before serving.

"Old Clothes" Braised Beef with Peppers and Onions

ROPA VIEJA

SERVES 6

There's a legend that a poor man, with nothing to feed his family, cooked old clothes, which his love transformed into a delicious stew now called Ropa Vieja. *Though closely associated with Cuban cuisine, both the story and accompanying dish actually come from the Canary Islands. The first mention of the recipe appears in the* Nuevo Manual del Cocinero Cubano y Español *(1857) under the title "*Ropa Vieja *a la Americana." Their use of* hierba buena *(spearmint) was interesting so I added it to the stock as well as the allspice and cloves favored in Oriente.*

FOR THE BRAISED BEEF

2 pounds flank steak or brisket, cut into 4 pieces

1 large yellow onion, quartered

1 large carrot, peeled and cut into 1-inch chunks

½ small red cabbage, quartered

½ small bunch fresh flat-leaf parsley, trimmed 1-inch above the stems, tender leaves reserved for garnish

2 sprigs fresh spearmint

4 large garlic cloves, peeled and crushed

1 teaspoon kosher salt

1 teaspoon whole black peppercorns

1 teaspoon whole allspice berries

½ teaspoon whole cloves

2 dried bay leaves

FOR THE *ROPA VIEJA*

¼ cup extra-virgin olive oil

1 large yellow onion, thinly sliced

1 large green bell pepper, stemmed, cored, seeded, and thinly sliced

4 large garlic cloves, peeled

1 teaspoon kosher salt

½ teaspoon freshly ground black pepper

½ teaspoon ground allspice

1 large pinch ground cloves

1½ cups Tomato Purée (page 304), or canned tomato purée

¼ cup dry white wine

1 dried bay leaf

1 cup roasted red peppers, sliced

Fresh flat-leaf parsley, leaves and tender stems, finely chopped

To prepare the braised beef, place the ingredients for the beef in a heavy 4- to 5-quart pot with 6 cups of water. Bring to a boil then reduce the heat to maintain a low simmer and cook, covered, until the beef is tender, 1½ to 2 hours.

Remove the pot from the heat and allow the beef to cool in the broth, so it will stay moist and juicy. Drain and set aside a ½ cup of the broth and reserve the remaining broth for future use. Remove the beef and when cool enough to handle, shred by hand, pulling apart its fibers with your fingers. Set the shredded beef aside.

To prepare the ropa vieja, heat the oil in a 10-inch skillet over medium heat. Add the onion and green pepper and sauté until the onion is soft and translucent, 6 to 8 minutes. Using a mortar and pestle, mash the garlic, salt, black pepper, allspice, and cloves to form a paste. Add the garlic paste to the skillet and continue to cook until fragrant, an additional 2 minutes. Add the reserved broth, tomato purée, wine, and bay leaf and return to a simmer. Stir in the shredded beef, reduce the heat to low, and cook, covered, 15 to 20 minutes. Stir in the sliced roasted red peppers and adjust the seasonings to taste. Sprinkle with freshly chopped parsley and serve over white rice.

Goat Stew

CHILINDRÓN DE CHIVO

SERVES 6 TO 8

Chef Dayron Ávila Alfonso says he learned to cook because he loved to eat. Not always happy with his mother's cooking, as a little boy he'd sneak into the kitchen and adjust the seasonings to his liking. His grandmother loved to teach him cooking tricks and together they'd make the rounds of the markets in their Marianao neighborhood. Now a chef in Vedado's Le Chansonnier, he gave me this Chilindrón de Chivo *recipe. After marinating overnight in red wine, the goat is seared then simmered in a red pepper* sofrito *over low heat until the goat is tender. For added spice, he sneaks in a little cinnamon at the end.*

3 pounds bone-in goat shoulder, trimmed of any excess fat and cut into 4-inch pieces

FOR THE MARINADE

2 cups red wine

½ large yellow onion, quartered

3 large garlic cloves, peeled and crushed

1 teaspoon kosher salt

1 teaspoon black peppercorns

1 teaspoon dried oregano

½ teaspoon whole cumin seeds, crushed

1 dried bay leaf

FOR THE STEW

½ cup grapeseed or canola oil

¼ cup extra-virgin olive oil

1 large yellow onion, diced

1 large red bell pepper, stemmed, cored, seeded, and diced

5 medium cachucha peppers (also known as *ajíes dulces*), diced

4 large garlic cloves, peeled and diced

1 teaspoon dried oregano

1½ teaspoons kosher salt

½ teaspoon freshly ground black pepper

½ teaspoon dried ground cumin

2 cups water

1½ cups Tomato Purée (page 304) or canned tomato purée

½ cup freshly squeezed sour orange juice or equal parts lime and orange juice

1 bunch fresh flat-leaf parsley, trimmed 2 inches above the stems and tied together with kitchen string (reserve the tender leaves for garnish)

1 whole cinnamon stick

1 dried bay leaf

1 cup pimiento-stuffed green olives, halved

1 to 2 tablespoons sherry vinegar

Place the goat in a large mixing bowl. To prepare the marinade, combine the wine, onion, garlic, salt, peppercorns, oregano, cumin seeds, and bay leaf in a small mixing bowl. Pour the marinade over the goat and marinate at least 2 hours or overnight in the refrigerator.

Remove the goat from the marinade and pat dry. Strain the marinade mixture, discard the solids, and set aside.

Heat the grapeseed oil in a 6-quart cast-iron or heavy-bottomed pot over medium-high heat until hot but not smoking. Working in batches, brown the goat pieces on all sides until the fat is rendered and the pieces are golden brown, 5 to 7 minutes. Do not overcrowd the pot and replenish the oil as needed. Set aside the browned pieces.

To prepare the *sofrito*, carefully remove the oil from the pot and wipe the pot clean. Heat the olive oil in the same pot over medium heat. Add the onion, red pepper, and cachucha peppers and sauté until the onion is soft and translucent, 6 to 8 minutes. Using a mortar and pestle, mash together the garlic, oregano, salt, black pepper, and cumin to form a smooth paste. Add the garlic paste to the *sofrito* and cook until fragrant, an additional 2 minutes.

Add the reserved marinade to deglaze the pot and bring to a hard simmer over medium-high heat for 10 minutes. Pour in the water, tomato purée, sour orange juice, parsley, cinnamon stick, and bay leaf and return to a hard simmer. Submerge the goat pieces in the pot so they are mostly covered. Return to a simmer then immediately lower the heat to medium-low and cook, covered, checking regularly and skimming the oil that rises to the top, until the goat is tender, 2 to 2½ hours.

Discard the parsley stems and stir in the olives. Add the vinegar and adjust the seasoning to taste. Garnish with freshly chopped parsley and serve.

NOTE

The goat should be as lean as possible but will release a good deal of fat as it cooks. The oil can be skimmed from the top in the final hour of cooking. The stew can also be prepared a day ahead then refrigerated. The fat will rise to the top and congeal and can then be easily removed.

Oxtail in Caper Sauce

RABO ALCAPARRADO

SERVES 6 TO 8

The sweetness of this Rabo Alcaparrado *is balanced out by a briny, caper-filled red-wine braising liquid kept at a low simmer until the oxtail is falling off the bone. I'm grateful to Rebecca Tembras-Bauza who shared her family's recipe with me.*

FOR THE OXTAIL

½ cup grapeseed or canola oil

3 pounds oxtail pieces, lean and trimmed of any excess fat

FOR THE *SOFRITO*

½ cup extra-virgin olive oil

1 large yellow onion, diced

1 large green bell pepper, stemmed, cored, seeded, and diced

4 large garlic cloves, peeled and diced

1½ teaspoons kosher salt

½ teaspoon freshly ground black pepper

½ teaspoon dried oregano

¼ teaspoon dried ground cumin

2 cups dry red wine, such as Cabernet Sauvignon or Pinot Noir

2 cups Beef Stock (page 306), or store-bought beef stock, plus more as needed

1½ cups Tomato Purée (page 304) or canned tomato purée

½ cup capers

1 bunch fresh flat-leaf parsley, trimmed 2 inches above the stems and tied together with kitchen string (reserve the tender leaves for garnish)

1 dried bay leaf

1 tablespoon sherry vinegar

Heat the grapeseed oil in a 6-quart cast-iron or heavy-bottomed pot over medium-high heat until hot but not smoking. Working in batches, brown the oxtail on all sides until the fat is rendered and the pieces are golden brown, 5 to 7 minutes. Do not overcrowd the pan and replenish the oil as needed. Set aside the browned oxtail. Carefully remove the oil and wipe the pot clean.

To prepare the *sofrito*, heat the olive oil in the same pot over medium heat. Add the onion, green pepper, and garlic and sauté until the onion is soft and translucent, 6 to 8 minutes. Add the salt, pepper, oregano, and cumin and cook until fragrant, an additional 2 minutes.

Add the red wine to deglaze the pot and bring to a hard simmer over medium-high heat for 10 minutes. Carefully pour in the stock, tomato purée, capers, parsley, and bay leaf and return to a fast simmer. Submerge the oxtails in the pot so they are mostly covered and bring back up to a simmer. Immediately lower the heat to medium-low and cook, covered, until the oxtails are tender, checking regularly and skimming the oil that rises to the top, 2 to 2½ hours.

Remove the parsley stems and discard. Add the vinegar and adjust the seasonings to taste. Garnish with freshly chopped parsley and serve.

Variation: **RABO ENCENDIDO | FIERY OXTAIL**

This version has a stronger tomato-based flavor and benefits from the added heat of fresh peppers. Add 1 to 2 teaspoons of minced habanero pepper with the onion and green pepper. Use 1 cup red wine and 2 full cups of tomato purée. Omit the capers or replace with sliced green olives.

Oven-Roasted Pork Shoulder

LECHÓN ASADO

SERVES 10 TO 12

From wild pigs fed on small nuts retrieved by ranch hands nimbly climbing royal palms to all day vigils around wooden roasting boxes, getting pork right is a serious Cuban affair. This Lechón Asado falls in between those extremes. The pork shoulder is marinated in mojo *then oven-roasted over several hours, usually overnight. The heat is cranked up at the very end until the skin turns a deep golden brown. Traditionally made for Nochebuena and served with trays of Moros y Cristianos (page 114) and Yuca con Mojo (page 225), it's a holiday dish that's simple enough to make for any occasion. This recipe comes from Sofía Benítez Otero.*

FOR THE MARINADE

2 cups freshly squeezed sour orange juice or equal parts lime and orange juice

1 whole head of garlic cloves, peeled

2 tablespoons kosher salt

1 tablespoon dried oregano

1 tablespoon freshly ground cumin (optional)

2 teaspoons freshly ground black pepper

7- to 8-pound bone-in, skin-on pork shoulder

1 cup freshly prepared Mojo Criollo (page 301)

Combine the ingredients for the marinade in a blender and process until smooth. Set aside until ready to use.

Place the pork in a large roasting pan. With the tip of a sharp knife, make numerous incisions into the meat (do not score the skin). Toss the marinade over the pork, cover with plastic wrap, and place in the refrigerator to marinate overnight, turning the meat several times if possible.

Preheat the oven to 250°F.

Bring the pork to room temperature. Remove the meat from the marinade, pat it dry, and reserve the marinade. Place the pork skin-side up inside the roasting pan and add the marinade back into the roasting pan. Cover the pork with aluminum foil and insert into the oven.

Cook for 8 to 9 hours until the meat reaches an internal temperature of 170°F to 190°F near the bone, shreds easily, and the liquid runs clear when the meat is pierced.

To get crisp skin, remove the pork from the oven and turn the oven up to 450°F. Once the oven is preheated, remove the foil from the pork and put it back in the oven. Check the pork every few minutes so the skin does not burn. Remove the pork when it has crisped nicely, 15 to 30 minutes total.

Remove the pork from the oven and let it rest 15 to 20 minutes before carving. Discard the braising liquid. Serve in chunks and drizzle with *Mojo Criollo* sauce.

Fried Pork Chunks

MASAS DE PUERCO

SERVES 6

This recipe is inspired by the Paladar de las Masas where we stopped on our way to Pinar del Río. The pork chunks are lightly salted, then set in a heavy pot with a small amount of lard and just enough water to cover. Kept at a gentle simmer the sounds of bubbling broth give way to a hard snap, indicating that the water has evaporated and the pork has rendered its lard. From there they begin to fry, browning and crisping on the outside, while staying pink and tender inside.

FOR THE PORK

3 pounds pork shoulder, cut into 4-inch chunks

1 tablespoon kosher salt

2 cups water

½ cup best-quality lard, at room temperature

FOR THE *MOJO*

6 large garlic cloves, peeled

1 teaspoon kosher salt

¼ teaspoon freshly ground black pepper

½ cup freshly squeezed sour orange juice or equal parts lime and orange juice

1 tablespoon fresh oregano, chopped

1 medium yellow onion, thinly sliced into rounds

Place the pork chunks in a heavy 6-quart pot. Salt the pork chunks and toss to coat well. Cover the pork with water and lard and stir to combine. Bring to a simmer then immediately reduce the heat to medium-low and cook partially covered until the water has reduced and the pork has rendered its lard, 1½ to 2 hours.

At this point the water will have mostly evaporated and the pork will begin to simmer in its own fat. Raise the heat to medium and continue to cook, uncovered, checking often and turning the pork regularly until the chunks are golden brown and crispy on the outside, 30 to 45 minutes. Remove the fried pork chunks with a slotted spoon and transfer to a serving platter. Carefully drain the rendered lard (about ½ cup) and set aside.

In the meantime prepare the *mojo*. Using a mortar and pestle, mash the garlic, salt, and black pepper to form a smooth paste. Whisk in the sour orange juice and oregano until well combined. Place the onion in a deep 12-inch skillet with a tight-fitting lid. Pour the *mojo* dressing over the onion and toss to coat. Cover the skillet.

Heat ½ cup of the rendered lard in a small saucepan. Bring to a simmer over medium heat. Remove the cover of the skillet away from your body and only enough to safely pour inside the lard in one motion then immediately cover the skillet. This should be done carefully because the liquid will bubble and spurt when it makes contact with the lard. Leave covered until the popping sound subsides, 3 to 5 minutes.

Spoon the onion over the pork chunks and toss to coat. Serve immediately.

Fresh Pork Sausages

BUTIFARRAS

MAKES 16 LINKS

Hearing Aida Palomo Camafreita describe her childhood spent on her family's farm just outside of Holguín, is like listening to a food fairy tale. Surrounded by her five sisters who loved to cook, instead of princes and pumpkins, they'd dream of the delicious lechoncito frito *they planned on making. Under their mother's direction, they'd take advantage of every part of the pig—from draining the blood for making* morcillas *(blood sausage) to frying pork cutlets in lard to preparing the casings for* butifarras, *and, on one occasion, a lovely pigskin suitcase.*

For her granddaughter Danielle Camafreita Álvarez, a classically trained chef who has done stints at the French Laundry and most recently at Chez Panisse, the joy her family takes in preparing food is a constant source of inspiration. Frequently consulting her grandmother, who at ninety-one still cooks daily, she re-created their recipe for butifarras—*diced pork shoulder seasoned with a large dose of* pimentón dulce, *cumin, and ground bay leaves. Sliced up and browned, it makes a wonderful breakfast, though Danielle's family most often serves it as an early-evening tapa alongside their usual cocktail hour whiskey.*

FOR THE *BUTIFARRAS*

3 pounds pork shoulder (preferably 70 percent lean meat), cut into 1-inch chunks

2 tablespoons *pimentón dulce* (Spanish-style sweet paprika)

1½ tablespoons kosher salt

1 tablespoon freshly ground black pepper

1 tablespoon ground cumin

4 dried bay leaves, finely ground

¼ to ½ pound back fat, diced by hand (optional)

2 ounces salted hog casings, soaked, rinsed, and cut into 2-foot lengths

FOR THE POACHING LIQUID

1 medium yellow onion, quartered

½ large green bell pepper, quartered

1 teaspoon whole black peppercorns

1 dried bay leaf

SPECIAL EQUIPMENT:

Stand mixer or meat grinder with ¼-inch plate disc; sausage stuffing nozzle or similar funnel (see note)

Pass the pork shoulder through a meat grinder fitted with a ¼-inch plate disc into a large mixing bowl. Add the *pimentón dulce*, salt, black pepper, cumin, and bay leaves and combine until mixed well. Add the diced fat only as needed to reach the desired 70 percent lean meat to 30 percent fat ratio.

To fill the sausages, knot the first length of hog casing at one end and bunch the rest of the casing over the sausage-stuffing nozzle. Place a large baking sheet under the stuffing nozzle. Hold the casings in place at the base of the nozzle and pass the mixture through the machine according to manufacturer's instructions. Ease off a little bit of the casing at a time as it fills up with the pork mixture, pinching off a link every 5 inches, until you have 4 sausages. Alternate the direction of each twist so that the links hold together. Do not cut into the links. Repeat with the remaining pork mixture and casings.

Prick each sausage in 2 to 3 places with a toothpick to prevent them from coming apart when they cook and to allow the flavorful poaching liquid to seep in.

To prepare the poaching liquid, fill a heavy 6- to 8-quart stockpot with water and add the onion, green pepper, black peppercorns, and bay leaf. Cover and bring to a hard simmer over medium-high heat. Add the linked sausages and immediately lower the heat to maintain a gentle simmer until the sausages are cooked through, 15 to 20 minutes. Remove the sausages and cool them in your refrigerator until firm, about 1 hour. At this point, the links can be separated, eaten as is, browned in a pan, or grilled.

NOTES

If you do not have a grinder, the pork shoulder can be purchased preground from a butcher then combined with the spices. Though a sausage-stuffing nozzle is preferable, any kind of metal nozzle or funnel can be used to fill the sausages.

The cooked links can be kept refrigerated, uncovered, for 3 to 4 days or wrapped and frozen for 4 to 6 weeks. Alternatively, fit the links into a glass jar or other container and cover with melted lard or olive oil to preserve them for up to 2 weeks in the refrigerator. They must be completely covered with fat to ensure their safe consumption.

CARNE DE CERDO ADOBADA

SERVES 6 TO 8

The recipe for this Carne de Cerdo Adobada *was given to me by Geraldo Alexander Palacios, a chef at Santiago's Academia Provincial de Artes Plásticas. The pork loin rests overnight in a sour orange adobo infused with garlic, oregano, and allspice then simmers on the stove top in an aromatic* sofrito. *Leftovers of this flavorful roast work beautifully in* Cuban sandwiches *(page 311).*

3 pounds boneless pork loin roast

FOR THE MARINADE

2 cups freshly squeezed sour orange juice or equal parts lime and orange juice

¼ cup white wine vinegar

1 small head of garlic

1 teaspoon dried oregano

1 teaspoon whole allspice berries

1 teaspoon kosher salt

½ teaspoon freshly ground black pepper

FOR THE *SOFRITO*

½ cup grapeseed or canola oil

¼ cup olive oil

1 large red onion, diced

3 scallions, trimmed and diced

3 small cachucha peppers (also known as *ajíes dulces*), stemmed, seeded, and minced

2 to 3 small *ajíes picantes* (or tabasco or cayenne peppers) stemmed, seeded, and minced

3 large garlic cloves, peeled and mashed

1 teaspoon whole cumin seeds, crushed

1 teaspoon kosher salt

½ teaspoon freshly ground black pepper

4 cups Chicken Stock (page 306), or store-bought chicken stock

½ cup dry white wine

¼ cup fresh oregano leaves, finely chopped

2 dried bay leaves

Trim the pork loin of any excess fat. With the tip of a sharp knife, make numerous deep incisions into the loin. Place the loin into a large mixing bowl or baking pan.

Combine the ingredients for the marinade in a blender and process until well combined. Pour the marinade over the pork loin, cover the bowl in plastic wrap, and refrigerate at least 2 hours or preferably overnight.

Remove the pork from the marinade, pat dry, and set aside. Heat the grapeseed oil in a 6-quart cast-iron or heavy-bottomed pot over medium-high heat until hot but not smoking. Brown the pork on all sides until the fat is rendered, 7 to 10 minutes. Set the pork loin aside.

To prepare the *sofrito*, carefully remove the grapeseed oil from the pot and wipe the pot clean. Heat the olive oil in the same pot over medium heat. Add the onion, scallions, cachucha peppers, and *ajíes picante* and sauté until the onion is soft and translucent, 6 to 8 minutes. Using a mortar and pestle, mash together the garlic, cumin, salt, and black pepper to form a smooth paste. Add the garlic paste to the pot and cook until fragrant, an additional 2 minutes.

Return the pork loin to the pot with the *sofrito* and add the chicken stock, wine, oregano, and bay leaves. Bring to a hard simmer over medium-high heat. Lower the heat to medium-low, cover, and continue to simmer until the roast is cooked through and an instant-read thermometer registers 140°F to 145°F, 30 to 40 minutes.

Transfer the pork loin to a cutting board and let rest before carving, about 10 minutes. Bring the remaining sauce in the pot to a hard simmer until reduced by half, 10 to 15 minutes. Serve the pork loin sliced with the sauce.

FISH
and
SEAFOOD

I knew it was a long shot when I set out to find Santi's sushi restaurant along the Jaimanitas River. I had made an appointment to meet him, but friends warned me that he was elusive. Getting lost along the way, it seemed less likely I'd find him at all with each wrong turn.

It was surprising that there is so little fresh fish available in Cuba. Difficult to procure and expensive, the quality of the fish served even in established restaurants is variable, while preserved *escabeche* and the ubiquitous bacalao have largely disappeared. There were bright spots— fish pulled directly from the water in the fishing villages surrounding the Bahía de Santiago, and coconut-drenched shrimp in Baracoa—but there were far more rare than you'd expect from a Caribbean island. The reasons I was given varied—from overfished waters and tight controls to boats that left and never came back.

This was hard to reconcile with my idea of the Cuban diet, which has always included dockside fritters served with yellow rice, weekly seafood *enchilados* poured over creamy cornmeal, and fresh snapper in every way imaginable. It made me more determined than ever to find Santi, but when I finally arrived, his daughter-in-law politely gave his excuses. I waited for a little while but I'm not sure how long. Watching a succession of mid-century cars cross the small bridge that took you back to the center of Havana, it felt like time wasn't passing at all.

PARGO RELLENO | *stuffed snapper* . . . 185

CAMARONES ENCHILADOS | *creole shrimp* . . . 189

HARINA CON CANGREJO | *cornmeal stew with crab* . . . 190

PESCADO EN SALSA DE COCO | *fish in coconut sauce* . . . 194

PESCADO FRITO CON MARIQUITAS |
fried fish with plantain chips . . . 196

MINUTAS CON ARROZ A LO SURGIDERO DE BATABANÓ |
breaded snapper and saffron rice . . . 201

FRITURAS DE BACALAO | *cod fish fritters* . . . 203

ESCABECHE | *pickled fish* . . . 204

Stuffed Snapper

PARGO RELLENO

SERVES 4 TO 6

María Luisa García shared the recipe for Pargo Relleno *she makes for her family. Simply marinated with a little bit of lemon juice, whole snappers are filled with shrimp, scallops, chives, and parsley then baked on a bed of potatoes that can be served as a hash on the side.*

2 pounds baby red or marble potatoes, scrubbed and halved

2 tablespoons olive oil

Two 1½- to 2-pound whole red or yellow tail snappers, scaled, gutted, gills removed, and slit down the middle

FOR THE MARINADE

4 large garlic cloves

1 teaspoon sea salt

¼ teaspoon freshly ground black pepper

½ cup freshly squeezed lemon juice

FOR THE FILLING

4 jumbo shrimp, peeled, deveined, and chopped

4 to 6 large sea scallops, small tendons removed and chopped

½ small yellow onion, finely chopped

¼ cup freshly squeezed lime juice

2 large garlic cloves, peeled and minced

1 tablespoon chives, chopped

1 tablespoon fresh flat-leaf parsley, leaves and tender stems, chopped

¼ to ½ cup bread crumbs

1 small orange, thinly sliced

Preheat the oven to 350°F.

Place the potatoes in a 13 x 8 x 3-inch ceramic baking dish. Drizzle the potatoes with 2 tablespoons of olive oil and sprinkle with salt and black pepper to taste. Toss the potatoes until they are well covered and the dish is lightly oiled. Set aside.

To prepare the marinade, use a mortar and pestle to mash the garlic, salt, and black pepper to form a smooth paste. Whisk in the lemon juice until well combined. Pour the marinade over each fish and rub with the seasonings both inside and out. Rest the fish in the refrigerator for 30 minutes.

To prepare the filling, combine the shrimp, scallops, onion, lime juice, garlic, chives, and parsley in a small mixing bowl. Add only enough bread crumbs to give the filling body and stir until well combined.

Stuff the belly of each fish with the filling. Lay 3 orange slices across each fish and use kitchen string to secure the orange slices to the fish and seal in the stuffing. Lay the fish side by side in the baking dish over the potatoes and drizzle with the remaining marinade. Place in the oven and bake uncovered until cooked through, about 1 hour.

Cut the strings and serve the fish whole or in fillets with the filling on the side. The potatoes can be served with the pan juices or cooked down further in the oven or a skillet to make a hash.

Creole Shrimp

CAMARONES ENCHILADOS

SERVES 4 TO 6

Though always spicy, Cuban food is rarely hot. Despite the name, there is very little "chili" in these shrimp—just a touch of diced habanero to give it some bite and justify its reputation.

2 pounds large shrimp, shelled and deveined

¼ cup freshly squeezed lime juice

1 teaspoon kosher salt

1 teaspoon freshly ground black pepper

¼ cup extra-virgin olive oil

1 large cubanelle (also known as Italian frying pepper), stemmed, seeded, and chopped

1 medium red onion, diced

4 garlic cloves, peeled and minced

1 cup diced tomatoes, fresh or canned

½ cup dry white wine

¼ teaspoon saffron threads

1 dried bay leaf

½ to 1 teaspoon fresh habanero pepper, stemmed and minced

1 cup red pimientos, drained and chopped

¼ cup fresh flat-leaf parsley, leaves and tender stems, finely chopped

¼ cup fresh cilantro, leaves and tender stems, finely chopped

Tabasco sauce

Place the shrimp in a large glass bowl. In a small bowl, mix together the lime juice, salt, and black pepper and pour over the shrimp. Allow the shrimp to marinate, covered, in the refrigerator for up to 2 hours. Drain the shrimp and reserve the marinade.

Heat the oil over medium heat in a deep 12-inch skillet. Add the green pepper, onion, and garlic and sauté until the onion is soft and translucent, about 5 minutes. Add the reserved marinade, tomatoes, wine, saffron, and bay leaf and bring to a simmer. Reduce the heat to low and simmer, covered, for 10 minutes. Add the habanero pepper to taste. Add the shrimp and pimientos and simmer, covered, until the shrimp are fully cooked, about 5 minutes. Remove the skillet from the heat and stir in the parsley and cilantro. Adjust the seasoning and sprinkle with Tabasco sauce to taste.

Cornmeal Stew with Crab

HARINA CON CANGREJO

SERVES 4 TO 6

In Harina con Cangrejo, *fresh crabmeat is added to a peppery* sofrito *with a touch of hot sauce then sprinkled with lime juice and poured over creamy cornmeal porridge. It is a particular favorite of the river goddess Oshún, represented by la Caridad del Cobre, Cuba's patron saint. Perhaps because of this* harina—*or yellow cornmeal, synonymous with hard times—is a cherished comfort food.*

FOR THE CORNMEAL

1½ cups coarse yellow cornmeal

Salt and freshly ground black pepper

FOR THE *ENCHILADA*

¼ cup extra-virgin olive oil

1 large green bell pepper, stemmed, cored, seeded, and diced

1 large red bell pepper, stemmed, cored, seeded, and diced

1 medium white onion, diced

4 large garlic cloves, peeled and minced

One 14.5-ounce can fire-roasted tomatoes, diced

1 tablespoon white wine vinegar

1 dried bay leaf

½ teaspoon sea salt

¼ teaspoon freshly ground black pepper

½ teaspoon *pimentón* (Spanish-style paprika)

¼ teaspoon ground celery seed

½ pound fresh lump crabmeat, picked through for shells and well drained

Tabasco or similar hot pepper sauce

Fresh lime wedges

Bring 6 cups of water to a boil in a heavy 5- to 6-quart pot. Add the cornmeal in a steady stream, whisking constantly until well blended so that no lumps form. Lower the heat to medium-low, stirring frequently until the cornmeal begins to pull away from the sides of the pot but is still creamy and smooth, 15 to 20 minutes. Add salt and black pepper to taste.

Heat the oil in a 12-inch skillet over medium heat. Add the green and red peppers, onion, and garlic and sauté until the onion is soft and translucent, 6 to 8 minutes. Add the tomatoes, vinegar, bay leaf, salt, black pepper, *pimentón*, and celery seed. Bring to a simmer and cook until the tomatoes begin to break down, about 10 minutes. Add the crab and warm until just heated through, 3 to 5 minutes. Adjust the seasonings to taste.

Divide the cooked cornmeal into individual bowls and top with the crab mixture. Sprinkle with Tabasco sauce or lime juice to taste.

WITH THEIR OWN FLEET OF FISHING BOATS
supplying their restaurant, there are many
sailors at Garcia's Seafood, but only one
captain. Though several of their recipes
started in her kitchen, María Luisa García
stayed at home raising children while her
husband, Esteban, built this community
mainstay along the Miami River. With
his passing, she joined her sons Esteban,
Jr., and Luis to help them run it. As the
authoritative calm amid the bustle of a
restaurant and fish market, she takes her
post at the front counter every day—cracking crab legs, weighing fish, and making
every single Cuban coffee that's ordered.
Friends, customers, and staff alike slow
their pace as they approach *la Señora,* as
she's known—lining up like children at their
first communion to make their requests or
just pay their respects. If they're patient,
they're rewarded with an approving smile,
reserved but warm. Generous with her
time and advice, she recited several of her
favorite recipes to me over an afternoon at
the restaurant. No matter how the recipe
started, it always ended the same way—
over *baja candela,* or low flame—which
she'd punctuate with a small sweep of her
hand that was straight from the hip. A
small reminder to always keep it steady.

Fish in Coconut Sauce

PESCADO EN SALSA DE COCO

SERVES 4

Geographically isolated in the Guantánamo province at the eastern-most point of the island, Baracoa is one of the few areas of Cuba with a claim to distinctly regional fare. This Pescado en Salsa de Coco, *made with fresh coconut milk seasoned with achiote, cachucha peppers, and culantro is a favorite.*

FOR THE FISH

Four 5-ounce white-flesh fish fillets, such as snapper, grouper, or sea bass

¼ cup freshly squeezed lime juice

Kosher salt

Freshly ground white pepper

FOR THE COCONUT SAUCE

2 tablespoons Achiote Oil (page 298)

5 small cachucha peppers (also known as *ajíes dulces*), stemmed, seeded, and diced

1 medium white onion, diced

4 large garlic cloves, peeled and mashed

1 teaspoon dried oregano

1 teaspoon kosher salt

½ teaspoon ground white pepper

¼ teaspoon ground cumin

2 cups fresh Coconut Milk (page 298) or best-quality canned unsweetened coconut milk

¼ cup lightly packed fresh culantro, finely chopped, plus more to garnish

Place the fillets in a glass baking dish. Pour the lime juice over the fillets then sprinkle with salt and pepper. Rest the fish in the refrigerator, for 30 minutes.

To prepare the coconut sauce, heat the achiote oil in a heavy 12-inch skillet over medium heat. Add the cachucha peppers and onion and sauté until the onion is soft and translucent, about 5 minutes. Using a mortar and pestle, mash the garlic, oregano, salt, white pepper, and cumin to form a smooth paste. Add the garlic paste to the skillet and sauté an additional 5 minutes. Add the coconut milk and culantro. Stir constantly until the sauce thickens slightly, 5 to 8 minutes. Adjust the seasonings to taste.

Remove the fillets from the marinade and add to the skillet skin-side up. Cover and cook over low heat until the fish is opaque and flakes easily when tested with a fork, 10 to 15 minutes. Baste the fish with the sauce. Garnish with additional culantro.

Variation: **MARISCOS CON SALSA DE COCO | SHELLFISH IN COCONUT SAUCE**

Prepare the coconut sauce as directed. After the initial simmer when the sauce has thickened, add 1 pound of large peeled and deveined shrimp, or 1 pound of jumbo lump crabmeat that has been picked over and coarsely shredded. Gently simmer over low heat until it is cooked through, 5 to 10 minutes.

Fried Fish with Fried Plantains

PESCADO FRITO CON MARIQUITAS

SERVES 2

Nestled in a fishing village in the keys surrounding Santiago Bay, El Marino *is a small* paladar *operated by the Yera family. Best known for their* enchilados *and whole fried fish served over a bed of* mariquitas, *everything gets a touch of* salsa picante—*a pepper-infused vinegar-based sauce made by the mother Ana Díaz Moreno. She kindly shared her recipe with me.*

One 1½- to 2-pound whole red or yellow tail snappers, scaled, gutted, and gills removed

4 large garlic cloves, peeled

1 teaspoon sea salt

¼ teaspoon freshly ground black pepper

2 tablespoons Salsa Picante (page 196) or fresh lime juice

½ cup canola or peanut oil

4 cups Mariquitas (page 311)

Place the fish in a 13 x 8 x 3-inch ceramic baking dish and score both sides of the fish with 3 evenly spaced slits halfway to the bone, about ¼ inch each.

Using a mortar and pestle, mash together the garlic, salt, and black pepper to form a smooth paste. Add the prepared *Salsa Picante* and stir until well combined. Rub the fish with the garlic paste both inside and out. Cover the baking dish with plastic wrap and set the fish in the refrigerator for 1 hour.

Heat the oil in a 14-inch wok over medium-high heat until hot but not smoking. Pat the fish dry. Lay the fish flat inside the wok so that the oil reaches halfway up the fish's belly. Fry the fish, basting the fish with the hot oil, until the belly becomes opaque, about 7 minutes on the first side. Flip the fish and fry on the other side until cooked through, 3 to 4 more minutes. Lay the fish on a serving platter and surround with *mariquitas* to serve.

SALSA PICANTE

MAKES 6 CUPS OF *SALSA PICANTE* CONCENTRATE

2 cups water

1 teaspoon turbinado sugar

1 medium yellow onion, diced

6 large whole garlic cloves, peeled

5 fresh cachucha peppers (also known as *ajíes dulces*)

5 small whole hot peppers, such as tabasco or cayenne

¼ cup whole allspice berries

¼ cup whole mixed peppercorns

4 cups white wine vinegar, plus more as needed

Combine the water and sugar in a small saucepan and bring to a boil until the sugar is dissolved, about 1 to 2 minutes. Allow to cool completely.

Combine the onion, garlic, cachucha peppers, hot peppers, allspice, and peppercorns in a 2-quart glass jar with a resealable lid. Stir in the sugar mixture concentrate and allow to marinate for 5 days then top off with white wine vinegar. Seal until ready to use.

Pour a ¼ cup of the above prepared concentrate in a small pint-glass jar and top off with additional white wine vinegar to make the prepared final sauce. Use the prepared sauce to marinate fish, chicken, or meat.

NOTE

The jar of *salsa picante* concentrate will keep well in a cool, dark place for 2 months or longer. Replenish with additional peppers and spices and top off with vinegar as it is used.

Breaded Snapper and Saffron Rice

MINUTAS CON ARROZ A LO SURGIDERO DE BATABANÓ

SERVES 8

Minutas con Arroz *is a childhood favorite of Clarita Díaz-Bergnes. Born in the fishing village of Surgidero de Batabanó, she spent afternoons helping her grandfather mend his nets with a giant wooden knitting needle. Her mother was an expert at preparing whatever fish came in and she often tucked breaded* minutas *into this saffron rice that was simmered with freshly made fish stock. It all seemed very far away when Clarita showed me how to make it in her sunny Miami high-rise apartment until I noticed that from every window she had a view of the ocean.*

FOR THE FILLETS

Eight 4- to 5-ounce snapper fillets or other white-fleshed fish, skinned

¼ cup freshly squeezed lemon juice

Sea salt

Freshly ground black pepper

4 extra-large eggs, well-beaten

2 to 3 cups dried bread crumbs or cracker meal

1 cup peanut oil, plus more as needed

FOR THE SOFRITO

¼ cup of extra-virgin olive oil

2 medium yellow onions, diced

2 medium green bell peppers, stemmed, cored, seeded, and diced

4 garlic cloves, peeled and mashed

1 teaspoon sea salt

¼ teaspoon freshly ground black pepper

2 teaspoons dried oregano

¼ teaspoon ground cumin

1 pinch red pepper flakes

FOR THE RICE

4 cups Fish Stock (page 307) or store-bought fish stock

2 cups Tomato Purée (page 304) or canned tomato purée

1 cup dry white wine

1 tablespoon apple cider vinegar

½ teaspoon saffron threads

3 cups Valencia or similar short-grain rice, rinsed

One 12-ounce bottle of pilsner-style beer

Pimientos

Place the fillets in a large glass baking dish. Pour the lemon juice over the fillets then sprinkle with salt and black pepper. Cover the dish and set in the refrigerator, 30 to 60 minutes.

Place the beaten eggs in a bowl and spread one cup of bread crumbs on a plate. Remove the fillets from the marinade and dip each fillet in the beaten eggs then coat in the bread crumbs, brushing off the excess crumbs. Repeat a second time until each fillet is completely covered, replenishing the bread crumbs as needed. Refrigerate the breaded fillets until ready to use.

Heat the peanut oil in a heavy 10-inch skillet over medium-high heat until hot but not smoking. Working in batches, add the breaded fillets to the skillet and fry until golden brown, about 3 to 4 minutes per side. Replenish with additional oil as needed. Transfer the fillets to a plate lined with paper towels.

To make the *sofrito*, heat the olive oil in a 6-quart heavy pot over medium heat. Add the onions, green peppers, garlic, salt, black pepper, oregano, cumin, and red pepper flakes and sauté until the onions are soft and translucent, 6 to 8 minutes. Stir in all but one cup of the fish stock, all of the wine, tomato purée, vinegar, and saffron and simmer for 10 minutes.

Stir in the rice and return to a fast simmer. Reduce the heat to the lowest possible setting and cook, covered, until the liquid is absorbed and the rice is tender, 25 to 30 minutes. Pour in the beer and the remaining fish stock and continue to cook an additional 10 minutes. The liquid should be partly absorbed but the rice should still be moist. Adjust the seasonings to taste.

Layer the prepared fillets inside the rice to warm through or serve alongside the rice so that the breading remains crisp. Garnish with pimientos.

NOTE

The fish stock can be made in advance then kept refrigerated for 3 to 5 days or frozen for up to 2 months. Allow to cool completely before storing. If using frozen fish stock, defrost in the refrigerator and proceed as directed.

Cod Fish Fritters

FRITURAS DE BACALAO

MAKES 16 FRITTERS

Though cod was once preserved in salt out of necessity, the distinctively briny flavor the process brings to an otherwise mild white fish makes these bacalao fritters very much a matter of choice.

1½ pounds boneless, skinless bacalao (dry salt cod), rinsed well

3 large eggs, well-beaten

1 small yellow onion, diced

¼ cup fresh flat-leaf parsley, leaves and tender stems, finely chopped

1 teaspoon baking powder

1 teaspoon sea salt

¼ to ½ cup unbleached all-purpose flour

2 cups grapeseed or canola oil

To desalt the cod, place the cod in a large heavy saucepan with cold water to cover. Bring to a slow simmer over medium heat for 15 to 20 minutes. Drain the cod and rinse with cold water. Test a small piece and repeat the process one more time, if needed, to reduce the saltiness. Transfer the cod to a mixing bowl and shred with a fork into small pieces

Stir in the egg, onion, parsley, baking powder, and salt. Gradually add the flour in spoonfuls until the mixture mounds on the spoon. Be careful not to overmix.

Heat 2 inches of oil over medium-high heat in a 4-quart heavy pot until a deep-fat thermometer registers 375°F.

Working in batches, carefully drop the batter in tablespoons until they are browned, turning once, 3 to 4 minutes total. Remove the fritters with a slotted spoon and drain on a plate lined with paper towels. Return the oil to 375°F in between batches. Serve immediately with Lime-Cilantro Vinaigrette (see page 74.)

Pickled Fish

ESCABECHE

SERVES 6

An Arab delicacy that found its way to Cuba via Spain, escabeche *was once a fixture in Miami's Cuban markets. The pickled fish drenched in an olive oil–and-vinegar marinade then set in an earthenware dish and left out for days has been quietly disappearing from the counters where it used to preside, though it's still made in homes. Served over white rice or crusty bread, it's a favorite during Lent and Holy Week leading to Easter. I was given this recipe by Margot Calzada.*

FOR THE FISH

Six 6-ounce kingfish or swordfish fillets, pin-bones removed and skinned

½ cup freshly squeezed lemon juice

Kosher salt

Freshly ground black pepper

1 cup unbleached all-purpose flour

1 cup extra-virgin olive oil

FOR THE PICKLING LIQUID

3 cups extra-virgin olive oil

3 large yellow onions, thinly sliced in rounds

3 medium green bell peppers, stemmed, cored, seeded, and thinly sliced

1 medium red bell pepper stemmed, cored, seeded, and thinly sliced

4 large garlic cloves, peeled and minced

1 cup pimiento-stuffed green olives, halved

1 teaspoon black peppercorns

2 dried bay leaves

1 cup white wine vinegar

½ teaspoon *pimentón* (Spanish-style paprika)

½ teaspoon achiote powder

Salt

Freshly ground pepper

To prepare the fish, place fillets in a 13 x 9 x 3-inch ceramic baking dish. Pour the lemon juice over the fillets and sprinkle with salt and pepper. Cover the fillets and marinate in the refrigerator overnight.

Place the flour in a large shallow bowl. Remove the fish from the marinade and pat dry. Dredge the fish in the flour. Heat ¼ cup of extra-virgin olive oil in a 12-inch nonstick skillet over medium-high heat. Cook each fillet, turning once, until cooked through, 3 to 4 minutes per side. Replenish with additional oil as needed. Place the fillets in a glass or ceramic baking dish to accommodate the fish in a single layer.

To prepare the pickling liquid, combine the remaining 3 cups of olive oil, onions, green and red peppers, and garlic in a 5- to 6-quart heavy pot. Bring to a simmer, cover, and cook over medium heat, 3 to 4 minutes. Add the olives, peppercorns, and bay leaves. Reduce the heat to low and continue to simmer 5 more minutes. Stir in the vinegar and simmer until the smell of vinegar abides, 3 to 5 minutes. Remove the pot from the heat and add the *pimentón* and achiote powder. Adjust the salt and pepper to taste.

Pour the prepared liquid over the fish fillets. Bring to room temperature, cover the dish, and marinate for 2 to 3 days. Serve at room temperature.

NOTE

Traditionally, *escabeche* does not need to be refrigerated. This recipe can be kept in a cool dry place for 2 to 3 days before serving. It can also be refrigerated for up to 1 week and served at room temperature.

FRUITS *and* VEGETABLES

Throughout the 1970s, Miami underwent a long process of colorization. One by one, fruits and vegetables native to Cuba took root throughout South Florida to meet the demands of a growing market. Guavas and carambolas, *guanábanas* and *fruta bomba*, appeared like long-lost relatives. Though it was largely completed by the time I was born, I remember my parents stopping the car at the sight of a mamey tree or the elaborate ceremony surrounding our introduction to fragile sapodillas. Less vibrant but no less important, root vegetables like yuca, malanga, and boniato are ever present. Most often, they are boiled and dressed in *mojo* or quickly fried—a legacy of the *frituras* brought from southern Spain with the earliest colonizers. Earthy Creole corn is blended with a *sofrito* and tender pieces of pork to make tamales, and calabaza brings a honeylike sweetness to every dish. Plantains are enjoyed in every stage of ripeness. Traveling through the Cuban countryside, seeing cacao trees, mangos *bizcochuelos* in full bloom, open fields of malanga, and chayotes hanging from vines and not forgotten in market bins, it was the same thrill in reverse.

ENSALADA DE AGUACATE | *avocado salad* . . . 211

TAMAL DE MAÍZ | *corn tamale* . . . 212

AGUACATE RELLENO | *stuffed avocado* . . . 214

FUFÚ DE PLÁTANO CON CHICHARRONES DE PUERCO |
mashed plantains with pork rinds . . . 215

PLÁTANOS SANCOCHADOS CON VINAGRETA DE LIMÓN |
simmered plantains with lime vinaigrette . . . 218

TOSTONES STUFFED WITH BEEF PICADILLO . . . 223

CALABAZA CON MOJO | *mojo with calabaza* . . . 224

FRITURAS DE CALABAZA | *calabaza fritters* . . . 228

FRITURAS DE MALANGA | *malanga latkes* . . . 231

Avocado Salad

ENSALADA DE AGUACATE

SERVES 4

The combination of avocado drizzled with olive oil and vinegar and tomatoes sprinkled with sugar to cut down the acidity makes this salad a sweet and tangy first course.

1 small vidalia or similar sweet onion, thinly sliced in rings

2 tablespoons white wine vinegar

1 tablespoon extra-virgin olive oil

1 medium ripe Florida avocado or 2 Hass avocados

Sea salt

Freshly ground black pepper

2 medium beefsteak tomatoes, cut into wedges

1 teaspoon sugar (optional)

1 small lime, quartered

Place the onions in a medium mixing bowl and toss with the vinegar and olive oil. Marinate the onions for 20 minutes.

Peel the avocado and cut into 1-inch chunks. Mound the avocado chunks in the center of a serving plate. Pour the dressed onions over the avocado and sprinkle with sea salt and pepper to taste. Place the tomatoes around the dressed avocado chunks and sprinkle the tomatoes with sugar. Serve with lime wedges.

Corn Tamales

TAMAL DE MAÍZ

MAKES 12 TO 14 TAMALES

When Apolonia "Poli" Bermúdez arrived in the United States in the early 1970s, a trip to the grocery store sent her home crying when she couldn't find the foods she missed. With her first Palacio de los Jugos in Little Havana, she started selling not only tropical fruits and vegetables but fresh juices, roasted pork, arroz congrí, chicharrones de puerco, *and golden tostones the size of sunflowers. She now operates six stores where no one ever leaves unhappy. Their Tamales de Maíz made with corn brought from their own farm are a personal favorite, and Poli shared her recipe with me.*

24 fresh or dried corn husks

6 ears dent or field corn, shucked and husks reserved (about 4 cups)

¼ cup best-quality lard

1 pound boneless pork shoulder, cut into ½-inch pieces

1 large yellow onion, diced

1 large red bell pepper, stemmed, cored, seeded, and diced

4 large garlic cloves, peeled and mashed

2 teaspoons kosher salt

½ teaspoon freshly ground black pepper

SPECIAL EQUIPMENT:

Tamalera or stockpot fitted with a steamer rack, kitchen string

To prepare the husks, bring a large 4- to 5-quart pot of water to a boil. Add the husks to the warm water and turn off the heat. Soak the husks until they are pliable, at least 30 minutes. Remove the husks from the water, pat dry, and set aside until ready to use.

Cut the kernels from the cobs and reserve the cobs for later use (see note). Put the corn kernels in a food processor and pulse until it forms a textured meal.

Melt the lard in a heavy 4-quart pot over medium-high heat. Add the pork and cook until lightly browned, 2 to 3 minutes. Add the onion, red pepper, garlic, salt, and black pepper and sauté until the onion is soft and translucent, 6 to 8 minutes. Reduce the heat to medium-low and simmer, covered, until the pork is tender, an additional 15 minutes. Stir in the ground corn and cook until warmed through, 2 to 3 minutes. Remove the pot from the heat and set aside until ready to use.

Place the prepared husks in front of you. Wrap the wide side of a husk around your hand to form an opening. Fold over the opposite end of the husk to form a hollow cup. Fill the cup with 3 to 4 tablespoons of corn mixture. Take a second husk and wrap the wide side around the seam side of the filled husk. Fold over the opposite end of the husk to close. This will create two interlocking cups. Tie the tamal with kitchen string. Repeat with the remaining husks and corn mixture.

Use a *tamalera* or place a steamer rack in the bottom of a large stockpot. Fill with enough water to reach the top of the rack. Add a dash of salt to the water and drop a nickel into the bottom of the pot before adding the tamales. If the water evaporates, the nickel will rattle and let you know to add more water.

Add the tamales to the pot with the open seam up. The tamales should not come in contact with the water. Cover tightly with a lid and set to a gentle boil over medium heat until the tamales are firm and pull away from the wrapper, 45 to 60 minutes. Replenish the water as needed. Remove the pot from the heat and leave the tamales covered for 10 minutes before unwrapping.

NOTES

As you shuck the corn, sort the husks by size for later use. The coarse outer leaves can be used to line the bottom of the steamer, the wide inner leaves with the curved bottoms to wrap the tamales, and the thin leaves closest to the kernels to cut into strips and tie the tamales.

The reserved cobs can be used to improvise a steamer rack. Line the bottom of the pot with the cobs and cover with loose husks. Add the water as directed and watch closely as it simmers so you can replenish the water as needed.

AGUACATE RELLENO

SERVES 2

This is a great cold dish to make on a hot day. The velvety flesh of oversized Florida avocados are perfect for filling. In addition to tuna, this recipe works well with cooked shrimp, crab, or chicken.

Two 5-ounce cans olive oil–packed tuna, drained

½ small vidalia or similar sweet onion, finely diced

½ medium green bell pepper, stemmed, cored, seeded, and finely diced

¼ cup red pimientos, finely diced

½ tablespoon extra-virgin olive oil, plus more as needed

Freshly squeezed lime juice from ½ large lime, plus more more as needed

1 large ripe Florida avocado or 2 ripe Hass avocados

Sea salt

Place the tuna in a medium mixing bowl. Add the onions, green pepper, and pimientos and mix until well combined. Toss with ½ tablespoon of olive oil and sprinkle with lime juice. Refrigerate until ready to serve.

Slice the avocado in half and peel. Place both halves and on a serving dish and drizzle with additional olive oil, lime juice, and sea salt to taste. Fill the cavity of each avocado with the prepared tuna.

Mashed Plantains with Pork Rinds

FUFÚ DE PLÁTANO CON CHICHARRONES DE PUERCO

SERVES 4

Perhaps the best known Afro-Cuban dish, fufú *is made by mashing plantains in a large, wooden, mortar and pestle called a* pilón. *Ranging from plain wood to intricately carved sets, they are often passed down in families.*

4 yellow plantains, ripe but still firm

6 large garlic cloves, peeled

1 teaspoon kosher salt

¼ teaspoon freshly ground black pepper

2 to 3 tablespoons freshly squeezed lime juice

Pork rinds and lardons from freshly made Chicharrones de Puerco (page 217)

SPECIAL EQUIPMENT:

Pilón, a wooden mortar and pestle for mashing plantains available online or at Latin American grocery stores, food mill, or food processor

Slice the plantains into 2-inch chunks with the peels on. Place the plantains in a heavy saucepan with enough cold water to cover. Bring to a rolling boil. Lower to medium heat and simmer, covered, until the plantains are tender and peeking out of the peel, 10 to 15 minutes. Drain the plantains, peel, and set aside.

Using a *pilón,* mash the garlic, salt, and black pepper to form a smooth paste. Add the plantains and lime juice to the *pilón,* mash until well combined. Add the pork lardons and work them into the mashed plantains.

Chop the prepared pork rinds and crumble over the plantains to serve.

Variation : MATAJÍBARO

MAKES 20 TO 24 *MATAJIBAROS*

Prepare the *fufú* as directed. Heat 2 cups of canola oil over medium-high heat in a 10-inch skillet to 375°F. Working in batches, scoop out a heaping tablespoon of the *fufú,* shape into a ball, and add to the oil. Turn until brown on all sides, about 2 minutes. Remove with a slotted spoon and drain on a plate lined with paper towels. Return the oil to 375°F in between batches. Repeat with the remaining *fufú.*

NOTE

If using a food processor or food mill, mash the plantains first then add the lardons and *chicharrones* separately.

CHICHARRONES DE PUERCO | PORK BELLY RINDS

Cubans are very particular about chicharrones de puerco. *Favoring the rind, they fry it in crisp chunks leaving only a small layer of fat for an extra pocket of flavor. Unfortunately the pop and burst that gives them that blistery skin also makes them a challenge to fry. I tried many techniques but finally settled on a process given to me by Zulema Cruz, who learned how to make* chicharrones *over a wood-burning fire on her grandfather's farm in Pinar del Río.*

Instead of frying the pork belly in whole chunks, she removes the top layer of pure white fat between the rind and meat called the empella, *dices it into tiny pieces, and renders the lard over high heat. The pork rind is then added to the lard and gently fried over medium-low heat until it turns a deep-golden color. The remaining meat can be diced into lardons and saved for later use or, as in this case, mashed into* fufú.

1 pound boneless pork belly, rind and fat intact

Kosher salt
Additional best-quality lard as needed

Using a sharp knife, slice the rind and top layer of fat from the meat. Scrape off any fat that is clinging to the skin and reserve the fat. Cut the rind into 2-inch squares with a knife or scissors, sprinkle with salt, and set aside.

Remove the next layer of fat between the rind and meat called the *empella*. Dice the fat into tiny pieces. Place a heavy 3- to 4-quart saucepan over medium-high heat, add the diced *empella*, and stir constantly until it has rendered its fat and only crisp brown bits remain. Strain the rendered lard, discarding the solids, and return to the pot.

Pat dry the reserved pork rinds. Heat the rendered lard over medium-low heat. Replenish with additional lard if needed. Add the pork rinds and cover with a mesh screen to prevent oil splatter. Fry the pork rinds until they are golden and the skin is firm, stirring frequently, 25 to 35 minutes. Transfer to a plate lined with papers towels.

Cut the remaining pork meat into 1-inch lardons and sprinkle with salt to cover. Remove all but 2 tablespoons of the rendered lard and return the pot to medium-high heat. Sauté the lardons until browned on all sides and cooked through.

Simmered Plantains with Lime Vinaigrette

PLÁTANOS SANCOCHADOS CON VINAGRETA DE LIMÓN

SERVES 4 TO 6

Gently simmered plantains are a wonderful alternative to fried maduros *and* tostones. *The plantains should be completely yellow with only a few black spots so they do not come apart. Becky Epelbaum Lusky adds finely chopped garlic to the oil then strains it out to make a delicate lime vinaigrette.*

4 ripe yellow plantains

4 large garlic cloves, peeled and diced

½ cup extra-virgin olive oil

¼ cup freshly squeezed lime juice

1 teaspoon kosher salt

¼ teaspoon freshly ground black pepper

Slice the plantains into 2-inch chunks leaving the peels on. Put the plantains in a heavy pot with enough cold water to cover. Bring to a rolling boil. Lower to medium heat and simmer, covered, until the plantains are tender and peeking out of the peel, 10 to 15 minutes. Drain and peel when cool enough to handle. Place the plantains in a large serving bowl.

Heat the olive oil in a 10-inch skillet over medium heat. Add the garlic and sauté until golden and fragrant, being careful that it doesn't burn or it will become bitter, 2 to 3 minutes. Strain the olive oil and discard the solids. Whisk in the lime juice, salt, and black pepper until well combined. Adjust the seasonings to taste. Pour over the plantains and serve.

TOSTONES STUFFED WITH BEEF PICADILLO

SERVES 6 TO 8

Wonderful to eat plain with sea salt, fried tostones can also be molded into small flower-shaped cups that hold a variety of fillings, such as this savory and sweet Picadillo Clásico *(page 157).*

3 large green plantains

2 cups grapeseed or canola oil

Sea salt

2 cups Picadillo Clásico (page 157)

SPECIAL EQUIPMENT:

Tostoneras are two wooden (or plastic) planks hinged together with a shallow curve on the inside that can be used to evenly mash plantains. Wooden *tostoneras* for making stuffed tostones are available online and in Latin American grocery stores.

Run each plantain under warm water before peeling. Using a sharp knife, trim the ends and score each plantain lengthwise along the peel. Remove the peel in sections. Cut the plantains into 2-inch chunks.

Heat the oil in a deep frying pan until hot but not smoking. Add the plantains in batches and fry until golden all around, 3 to 5 minutes.

Test for doneness by placing one piece in the *tostonera* and smashing to the desired thickness. The plantain should spread out evenly but hold together from the center. Repeat with the remaining plantains then drain on a plate lined with paper towels.

Refry the plantains a second time until evenly crisp. Drain again and add sea salt to taste. Fill each plantain cup with a heaping spoon of picadillo.

NOTES

If not frying immediately, the plantains can be peeled then placed in a large mixing bowl with water to cover and 1 tablespoon of lime juice to prevent discoloration. Drain the plantains well and pat dry before proceeding to avoid oil splatter.

Mojo with Calabaza

CALABAZA CON MOJO

SERVES 8 TO 10

This Calabaza con Mojo *came from a chef working at one of the better-known restaurants in the Vedado section of Havana. I visited with family friends and enjoyed the meal so much that we asked to speak to the owner. Since it was a state-run restaurant, they laughed and told us he lived very far away and we had almost no chance of being granted an interview. I made a plan to meet with the chef the next day but he nervously told me he could only speak to me off the record, a pretty common occurrence in Cuba, even in the most seemingly benign situations. Though a little disappointed, we had a pleasant conversation. In the end, he threw out this suggestion at the last moment, leaving me without his name but with a lovely recipe.*

FOR THE CALABAZA

2 pounds calabaza (also known as West Indian Pumpkin), kabocha, or hubbard, seeded and sectioned into wedges 1 inch thick

FOR THE *MOJO*

6 large garlic cloves, peeled

1 teaspoon kosher salt

¼ teaspoon freshly ground black pepper

½ cup freshly squeezed sour orange juice or equal parts lime and orange juice

2 tablespoons fresh oregano leaves, finely chopped

1 large yellow onion, thinly sliced into rounds

½ cup extra-virgin olive oil

Place the calabaza on a steamer rack set inside a saucepan and steam over simmering water until tender, about 20 minutes. Transfer the calabaza to a large serving dish.

In the meantime, prepare the *mojo*. Using a mortar and pestle, mash the garlic, salt, and black pepper to form a smooth paste. Whisk in the sour orange juice and oregano until well combined.

Place the onions in a deep 12-inch skillet with a tight-fitting lid. Pour the *mojo* over the onions and toss to coat.

Heat the olive oil in a small saucepan. Bring to a simmer over medium heat. Remove the cover of the skillet away from your body and only enough to safely pour inside the hot oil in one motion then immediately cover the skillet. This should be done carefully because the juice will bubble and spurt when it makes contact with the oil. Leave covered until the popping sound subsides and the onions are steamed, 3 to 5 minutes.

Pour the *mojo* and simmered onions over the calabaza and serve immediately.

Variation: YUCA CON MOJO

Replace the calabaza with 3 pounds of fresh or frozen yuca cut into 2-inch chunks. Place the yuca in a 4-quart heavy pot with 1 tablespoon of salt and water to cover. Bring the yuca to a hard boil then immediately lower the heat to maintain a gentle simmer. Cover and cook the yuca until tender, 20 to 25 minutes. Drain the yuca, then slice in half and remove the fibrous core. Prepare the *mojo* as directed and drizzle over the yuca. Garnish with crumbled *Chicharrónes de Puerco (page 217)*.

Calabaza Fritters

FRITURAS DE CALABAZA

MAKES 34 FRITTERS

Frituras de Calabaza *caramelize the moment they touch the oil. The water content of the calabaza varies wildly so the purée should be drained well so the fritters hold their shape. I was given this recipe by Olga Marcos and always associate their burnt orange color to her red earth descriptions of Ciego de Ávila, where she grew up.*

4 pounds calabaza (West Indian pumpkin), rinsed, peeled, and cut into large pieces

1 extra-large egg, well-beaten

1 tablespoon sugar

1 teaspoon kosher salt

1 teaspoon baking powder

½ to 1 cup unbleached all-purpose flour

2 cups grapeseed or canola oil

Place the calabaza on a steamer rack set inside a saucepan and steam over simmering water until tender, about 20 minutes. Drain immediately and place in a large mixing bowl.

Mash the calabaza with a fork to form a textured paste. Drain off the excess water using a fine mesh sieve and return to the large mixing bowl. Stir in the egg, sugar, salt, and baking powder. Slowly add the flour in spoonfuls until the mixture mounds on the spoon. Do not overmix. Cover and chill in the refrigerator, at least 30 minutes.

Heat 2 inches of oil over medium-high heat in a 4-quart heavy pot until a deep-fat thermometer registers 375°F.

Working in batches, carefully drop the batter in tablespoons until they are browned and float to the top, turning once, 3 to 4 minutes. Remove the fritters with a slotted spoon and drain on a plate lined with paper towels. Return the oil to 375°F in between batches.

Sprinkle with salt and serve immediately.

Malanga Latkes

FRITURAS DE MALANGA

MAKES 14 TO 16 FRITTERS

As members of the small Sephardic community in Santiago, Mariana and Pepito Rivera knew of each other when they were young, but it wasn't until they reconnected in the United States that they started what they called a lifelong honeymoon. Adapting to the American celebration of Chanukah, Mariana added a Cuban touch to their holidays with these malanga *latkes. With roots going back to the sixteenth century, Pepito joked that they were the first Jewish family in Cuba. Their granddaughter Jennifer makes them now and shared the recipe with me.*

2 pounds *malanga*, peeled and cut into 2-inch chunks

1 medium yellow onion, quartered

1 extra-large egg, well-beaten

4 large garlic cloves, peeled and minced

¼ cup freshly squeezed lime juice

3 tablespoons fresh flat-leaf parsley, leaves and tender stems, finely chopped

1 teaspoon white vinegar

1 teaspoon kosher salt

½ teaspoon dried oregano

¼ teaspoon ground cumin

¼ teaspoon freshly ground black pepper

¼ to ½ cup olive oil

Sliced avocado to serve

Using a box grater or food processor fitted with a shredding disc, grate the *malanga* and onion. Place the grated vegetables in a large mixing bowl and stir in the egg, garlic, lime juice, parsley, vinegar, salt, oregano, cumin, and black pepper. Mix until well combined. Refrigerate until thickened, at least one hour.

Heat ¼ inch of oil over medium-high heat in a 10-inch skillet until hot but not smoking. Working in batches, spoon ¼ cup of the batter into the skillet and spread with a fork to form a 3-inch patty. Fry until golden on both sides, 2 to 3 minutes per side. Repeat with the remaining batter.

Transfer the fritters to a plate lined with paper towels. Serve immediately or keep the fried latkes in a warming oven preheated to 200°F. Serve with sliced avocado and sprinkle with lime juice.

SWEETS
and
DESSERTS

"This might be too much." *That's what I usually say to someone when I'm presenting* them with a Cuban dessert. Whether it's by way of explanation or warning, I don't know. What I do know is that pearly meringues and soothing custards, flans dripping in burnt sugar, and chocolate so thick that a churro stands up in it, can be everything that's good about being too much.

MERENGUITOS DORMIDOS | *sleeping meringues* . . . 237

NATILLA | *egg custard* . . . 240

ARROZ CON LECHE | *rice pudding* . . . 242

YEMITAS . . . 243

CAPUCHINO CAKE . . . 244

FLAN DE LECHE . . . 247

FLAN: COCO, QUESO, CALABAZA . . . 248

BUÑUELOS DE ANÍS CON ALMÍBAR | *anise fritters with syrup* . . . 250

TARTE TENTACIÓN | *ripe plantain tart* . . . 253

PAN DE MAÍZ CON COCO Y GUAYABA | *cornmeal cake with coconut and guava* . . . 256

CAKE CUBANO | *cuban layer cake* . . . 258

DULCE DE TOMATE | *tomato jam* . . . 261

DULCE DE COCO | *sweetened coconut* . . . 262

CUCURUCHOS DE COCO Y ALMENDRAS | *coconut and almond candy cones* . . . 265

CASQUITOS DE GUAYABA | *poached guava shells* . . . 266

MANTECADO | *cuban vanilla ice cream* . . . 270

FRUIT ICE CREAMS: CHERIMOYA, COCONUT, STRAWBERRY, MAMEY . . . 275

BAKED CHOCOLATE ICE CREAM "EL CARMELO" . . . 278

CHOROTE CON CHURROS | *hot chocolate with churros* . . . 281

Sleeping Meringues

MERENGUITOS DORMIDOS

MAKES 48 SMALL MERINGUES OR 32 LARGE MERINGUES

To make these sleeping meringues, place them inside a blazing-hot oven then immediately turn the oven off and leave them to bake overnight. The outside crisps up while the center stays soft and chewy. I was given this recipe by my friend María Budet who acted as her grandmother's puntista *when they made them together, dropping a teaspoon into the freshly whipped meringue then pulling it up to make sure it formed a tail and was at the right point to be piped.*

5 large egg whites (¾ cup) at room temperature

1½ cups sugar

1 teaspoon lime juice

Preheat the oven to between 400°F and 450°F (see note). Line two 13 x 18 x 1-inch baking sheets with parchment paper or a nonstick liner.

Using a hand beater or stand mixer fitted with the whisk attachment, beat the egg whites on low speed until foamy, about 1 minute. Increase the speed to medium-low and add the sugar one tablespoon at a time until the meringue holds soft peaks, about 5 minutes. Add the lime juice. Gradually increase the speed to high and continue to beat the meringue until it forms glossy, firm peaks, an additional 3 to 5 minutes.

Using a pastry bag fitted with the star attachment, pipe the meringues onto the prepared baking sheets in the desired shape or drop small mounds onto the sheet with a spoon.

Place both baking sheets into the preheated oven, close the door, and immediately turn the oven off. Leave the oven unopened for at least 8 hours or up to 12 hours.

NOTE

The oven should be preheated to 400°F for small meringues and 450°F for larger meringues. Prepare all the baking sheets before opening the oven. Once it is preheated, it should only be opened once to insert all the baking sheets at once.

Egg Custard

NATILLA

SERVES 8

Armed only with our grandmother's list of ingredients with no indication of how she put them together, for years my sister Carmen and I took turns attempting her natilla *to no avail. We'd come close but fall short of the smoothly rich custard she made so effortlessly. Finally, scribbled as a side note among her niece's papers, I found the full recipe. Contrary to what I knew about making custard, the ingredients are beaten together cold then strained and simmered. With a wooden spoon in hand, my sister followed the new directions and suddenly there it was, just as we remembered it. The next morning, I was relieved to see the* natilla *still in the fridge, half expecting it to have disappeared again.*

4 cups whole milk at room temperature

4 large egg yolks

1 cup sugar

4 tablespoons cornstarch

⅛ teaspoon kosher salt

1 whole cinnamon stick

One 2-inch strip of lime peel

1 teaspoon pure vanilla extract

Ground cinnamon

Combine the milk, egg yolks, sugar, cornstarch, and salt in a mixing bowl and whisk until the mixture is well combined and there are no visible yolks.

Pass the milk mixture through a fine-mesh sieve into a 3- to 4-quart saucepan. Add the cinnamon stick and lime peel and cook over medium heat, stirring constantly with a wooden spoon, until it thickens slightly, about 15 minutes. Lower the heat to medium-low, stir in the vanilla, and continue to stir until it coats the back of the spoon, an additional 5 to 7 minutes. Remove the saucepan from the heat and set aside.

Pour the custard into individual bowls or ramekins while still warm. Sprinkle with cinnamon to taste. Bring the custard to room temperature then chill in the refrigerator until set, at least 2 hours. The custard can be kept chilled in the refrigerator for up to 3 days.

ARROZ CON LECHE

SERVES 4 TO 6

I was given this Arroz con Leche *recipe by my friend Anna Christie from her great-aunt Dora Áloma who always had a bowl waiting for her, lime peels and all, when she went to visit. The rice is left to soak overnight then boiled twice, first in water then in milk, becoming richer and creamier with each step.*

½ cup Valencia or similar short-grain rice, rinsed

2 cups water

⅛ teaspoon kosher salt

4 cups whole milk

4 whole cinnamon sticks

½ cup sugar

1 teaspoon pure vanilla extract

Peel of 2 large limes taken off in long strips

Ground cinnamon

Soak the rice in a heavy 4-quart pot with water to cover, 8 hours or overnight.

Drain the rice and return to the pot with 2 fresh cups of water and salt and bring to a boil. Reduce the heat to medium and simmer until the rice is moist but has absorbed most of the liquid, 10 to 12 minutes. Stir in the milk and cinnamon sticks and return to a boil. Reduce the heat to medium and continue to simmer, stirring frequently, until the rice is tender and creamy, 25 to 30 minutes. Stir in the sugar, vanilla, and lime peel. Reduce the heat to low and simmer, stirring constantly, an additional 10 minutes.

Remove the lime peel and discard. Pour the pudding into a large serving bowl or individual ramekins while still warm. Sprinkle with cinnamon to taste. Bring to room temperature then chill in the refrigerator until set, at least 2 hours. The pudding can be kept refrigerated for up to 3 days.

YEMITAS

MAKES 36

Little more than egg yolks and syrup beaten into a creamy paste and rolled in powdered sugar, yemitas *are a sentimental favorite at Cuban bakeries. They are delicate, demure, and hard to get right. Fortunately, pastry chef Lucila Venet-Jiménez was a very good student. As a little girl, she attended adult cooking classes in her Vedado neighborhood, taking her spot in the very first row. At home, she and her mother watched their favorite cooking show hosted by Ana Dolores Gómez de Dumois. As a young wife and mother herself, Lucila signed up for classes taught by Ana Dolores in her Miami home and became the youngest person in the room once again. While the other ladies gossiped, she and Ana Dolores would get to work. Stumped by* yemitas, *they were joined by esteemed Cuban food writer Dolores Alfonso y Rodríguez and the three of them worked out this recipe, which Lucila shared with me.*

2 cups sugar

1 cup water

¼ teaspoon freshly squeezed lime juice

16 large egg yolks, lightly beaten

1 teaspoon pure vanilla extract

1 cup confectioners' sugar, sifted

SPECIAL EQUIPMENT:

4-quart copper pot or heat safe copper mixing bowl

Combine the sugar, water, and lime juice in a medium saucepan and bring to a boil. Simmer over medium heat until it reaches the thread stage and registers 230°F on a candy thermometer, 10 to 15 minutes. Set aside and cool to room temperature before proceeding.

Place the egg yolks in a heat-safe copper pot. Stir in the cooled syrup and whisk until well combined. Place over medium-low heat and stir by continually working a wooden spoon backward and forward until you can see the bottom of the pot, 30 to 35 minutes. Remove the pot from the heat and stir in the vanilla. Pass the *yemitas* through a fine-mesh sieve onto a marble slab or baking sheet lined with wax paper, cover with a damp cloth until cooled completely.

Place the confectioners' sugar in a small mixing bowl. Scoop up 1 teaspoon of *yemita* and shape into a ball then roll in the sugar. Place the finished *yemitas* on a tray lined with clean parchment paper or paper candy cups. *Yemitas* can be kept at room temperature for 2 days or refrigerated for 1 week.

CAPUCHINO CAKE

SERVES 8 TO 10

This Capuchino Cake *is inspired by the bright yellow conelike cakes wrapped in frilly white paper sold at Cuban bakeries. Taking their name from the pointy hats worn by Capuchin monks, they are difficult to shape and require tricky specialized molds. Margot Coro developed this recipe as an alternative, which her daughter-in-law shared with me. The eggs yolks are beaten over an extended period of time then baked in a single cake pan. Before the cake is fully removed from the oven, it is drenched in spiced syrup and served chilled or covered in meringue.*

12 extra-large egg yolks

2 extra-large egg whites

2 tablespoons cornstarch, sifted

4 cups of sugar

2¼ cups water

1 whole cinnamon stick

Meringue Topping (page 245)

Preheat the oven to 300°F. Butter a 10-inch cake pan, then dust with flour and set aside.

In a stand mixer fitted with the whisk attachment, beat the egg yolks and egg whites on medium speed until thick and creamy, 25 minutes. Slowly add the cornstarch and continue to beat an additional 5 minutes.

Pour the egg mixture for the cake into the prepared pan. Place in the preheated oven and bake for 35 minutes.

In the meantime, prepare the sugar syrup. Combine the sugar, water, and cinnamon stick in a large pot. Simmer over medium heat until the sugar is dissolved, about 5 minutes.

When the cake is baked but still in the oven, pull out the rack and drizzle the cake with 3 tablespoons of syrup. Remove the cake from the oven and pierce the cake in several places with a cake tester or skewer. While still warm, pour the remaining syrup over the cake. Please note, the syrup must be added immediately after the cake is taken from the oven or it will not be able to absorb the syrup.

Allow the cake to cool completely then cover and refrigerate until cold, at least 2 hours.

To unmold, run a sharp wet knife along the border. Place a serving plate over the cake and flip in one motion. Allow to slowly drop on the plate. Decorate with prepared Meringue Topping.

MERINGUE TOPPING

3 egg whites

Pinch cream of tartar

¾ cup sugar

½ teaspoon pure vanilla extract

In a stand mixer fitted with the whisk attachment, beat the egg whites on low speed until foamy, about 1 minute. Add the cream of tartar and increase the speed to medium until they hold soft peaks. Gradually add the sugar followed by the vanilla extract and beat on high speed until it forms stiff, glossy peaks, about 5 more minutes.

FLAN DE LECHE

SERVES 8 TO 10

The trick to a great Flan de Leche *begins and ends with the* caramelo—*the sugar heated slowly over a steady flame until it reaches just the right amber hue without becoming bitter. It can get away from you easily, but it's always fun to see how far you can take it.*

FOR THE MOLD

¾ cup sugar

FOR THE CUSTARD

2½ cups whole milk

One 12-ounce can evaporated milk

1½ cups sugar

1 whole cinnamon stick

1 whole vanilla bean, split lengthwise, or
    1 tablespoon pure vanilla extract

1 lemon peel, white pith removed

⅛ teaspoon kosher salt

6 large eggs

SPECIAL EQUIPMENT:

7- to 8-inch *flanera* or round metal cake
    pan (preferably 3 inches deep)

Preheat the oven to 350°F.

Pour ¾ cup of sugar into a *flanera* or metal mold. Place the mold over medium heat and move constantly, without stirring, until the sugar melts and takes on a deep amber hue, 5 to 8 minutes. Remove the mold from the heat and swirl the caramel so that the bottom and sides are lightly covered. The caramel will be very hot and should be handled carefully. Set aside.

Combine the whole milk, evaporated milk, sugar, cinnamon, vanilla bean, lemon peel and salt in a heavy 4-quart saucepan and bring to a boil over medium heat. Remove the saucepan from the heat and allow the spices to steep until the milk is cooled to room temperature, about 30 minutes. Discard the cinnamon, vanilla bean, and lemon peel.

Combine the cooled milk mixture and eggs in a mixing bowl and whisk until well combined. Carefully pour the custard into the prepared mold. Close the lid of the *flanera*, if using, or cover the mold with aluminum foil.

Prepare a *baño de María*. Place the filled mold in a larger roasting pan. Pour enough hot water into the pan so that it comes about halfway up the sides of the mold. Carefully place both pans in the oven and bake for 60 to 75 minutes, until a knife inserted into the center comes out clean. Allow the custard to cool completely then refrigerate, covered, at least 4 hours or overnight.

To unmold, run a thin knife along the side of the mold. Gently shake the mold to loosen the flan. Place a large plate over the flan and quickly invert the mold in one motion. The flan will gently drop onto the plate and the caramel will flow out.

FLAN DE COCO

SERVES 8 TO 10

It's always strange when I see flan listed as a special on a dessert menu. Far from specialized in Cuban restaurants, it's not rare to find an all-flan lineup—de leche, de queso, de calabaza, and of course—de coco. The shredded coconut in this flan rises to the top, creating a bottom layer of custard-soaked coconut flakes when the flan is inverted. I was given this recipe by my great-aunt Olga Bufill and the same ratios can be used to make a variety of flans.

¾ cup sugar

One 14-ounce can sweetened
    condensed milk

One 12-ounce can evaporated milk

5 large eggs

1 tablespoon pure vanilla extract

Pinch kosher salt

1½ cups Dulce de Coco (page 262) or
    canned shredded coconut, well-drained

SPECIAL EQUIPMENT:

7- to 8-inch *flanera* or round metal cake
    pan (preferably 3 inches deep)

Preheat the oven to 350°F.

Pour the sugar into a *flanera* or metal mold. Place the mold over medium heat and move constantly, without stirring, until the sugar melts and takes on a deep amber hue, 5 to 8 minutes. Remove the mold from the heat and swirl the caramel so that the bottom and sides are lightly covered. The caramel will be very hot and should be handled carefully. Set aside.

To prepare the custard, combine the condensed milk, evaporated milk, eggs, vanilla, and salt in a blender. Process on the lowest setting until well blended and pour into a large mixing bowl. Stir in the drained coconut until well combined. Carefully pour the custard into the caramelized mold. Close the lid of the *flanera*, if using, or cover the mold with aluminum foil.

Prepare a *baño de María*. Place the filled mold in a larger roasting pan. Pour enough hot water into the pan so that it comes about halfway up the sides of the mold. Carefully place both pans in the oven and bake for 60 to 75 minutes, until a knife inserted into the center comes out clean. Allow the custard to cool completely then refrigerate, covered, at least 4 hours or overnight.

To unmold, run a thin knife along the side of the mold. Gently shake the mold to loosen the flan. Place a large plate over the flan and quickly invert the mold in one motion. The flan will gently drop onto the plate and the caramel will flow out so allow extra space around the flan.

Variation: FLAN DE QUESO

Add 8 ounces of softened cream cheese to the custard before blending. Proceed with the recipe as directed.

Variation: FLAN DE CALABAZA

Add 8 ounces of softened cream cheese and 1 cup canned or fresh calabaza or pumpkin purée to the custard before blending. Proceed with the recipe as directed.

NOTE

As an alternative, the caramel can be done separately in a small saucepan than poured into the mold.

BUÑUELOS DE ANÍS CON ALMÍBAR

MAKES 12 TO 14 *BUÑUELOS*

Rosa Rodríguez-Duarte learned to cook at an early age. Left at home alone, her father would push a small bench up to the counter so that she could reach anything she might need. Among her favorite recipes was this one for buñuelos, *seasoned with whole anise seeds, which she still makes for her family on Nochebuena.*

FOR THE *BUÑUELOS*

½ pound yuca, peeled and cut into 1-inch chunks

¼ pound boniato, peeled and cut into 1-inch chunks

¼ pound malanga, peeled and cut into 1-inch chunks

¼ pound ñame, peeled and cut into 1-inch chunks

1 tablespoon kosher salt

1 teaspoon whole anise seeds

¼ pound calabaza, peeled and cut into 2-inch chunks

3 large eggs, well-beaten

3 to 4 cups unbleached all-purpose flour

2 cups canola oil or grapeseed oil

FOR THE SYRUP

2 cups water

1 cup sugar

1 whole star anise

1 whole cinnamon stick

One 3-inch strip lime zest, white pith removed

1 to 2 tablespoons freshly squeezed lime juice

Place the yuca, boniato, malanga, ñame, salt, and anise seeds in a heavy pot with cold water to cover. Bring to a boil then lower the heat to medium and simmer, covered, for 10 minutes. Add the calabaza and simmer until all the vegetables are tender. Drain well.

Force the vegetables through a ricer or food mill onto a lightly floured surface while the vegetables are still warm. Gather the puréed vegetables into a mound and form a well in the center. Pour the beaten eggs into the well and knead into the vegetables. Sift the flour over the mixture and blend, a little bit at a time, until it forms a smooth dough that holds together.

Cut the dough into 14 pieces. Roll each piece of dough into rope about a ½ inch thick and shape into a figure eight.

Heat the oil over medium-high heat in a 10-inch skillet to 375°F. Working in batches, fry the *buñuelos*, until they are golden on each side, 3 to 4 minutes. Transfer to a plate lined with paper towels to drain.

Prepare the syrup. Combine all the ingredients except for the lime juice in a saucepan and bring to a boil. Simmer until it reaches a syruplike consistency, 15 to 20 minutes. Off heat, add lime juice to taste. Serve with the fried *buñuelos*.

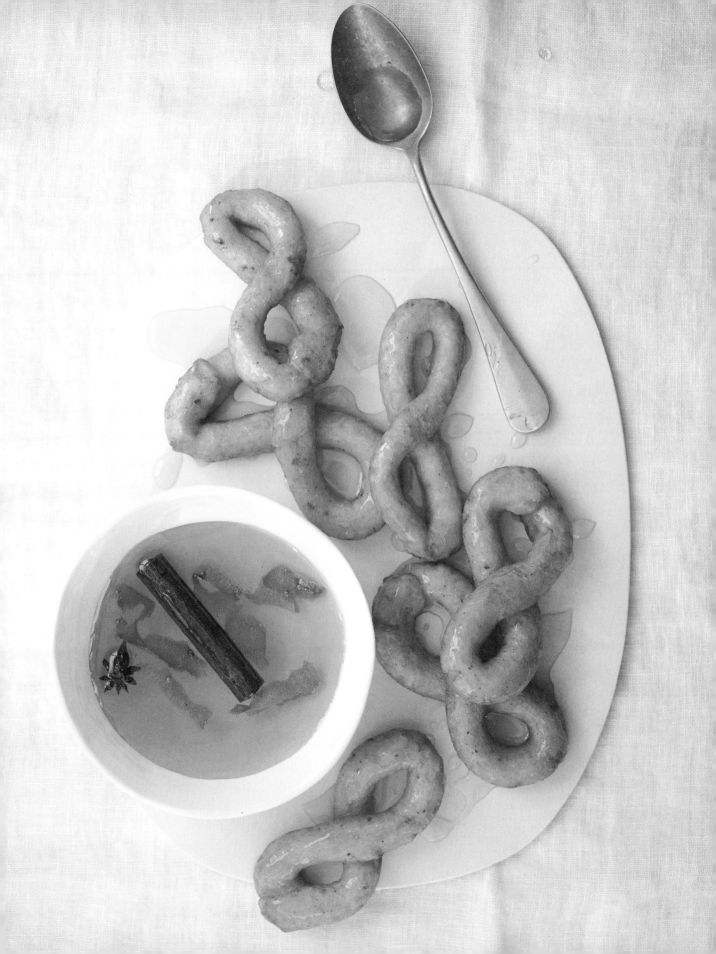

Ripe Plantain Tart

TARTE TENTACIÓN

SERVES 4 TO 6

Just like the apples in a tarte tatin, plantains can never be too dark or sweet, the blackened bits adding an extra layer of smoke to the caramel. For this Tarte Tentación, *plantains are sprinkled with sugar, cinnamon, and rum then baked under a flaky, butter crust.*

FOR THE CRUST

1¼ cups unbleached all-purpose flour

½ teaspoon kosher salt

1 tablespoon sugar

10 tablespoons (1¼ sticks) unsalted butter, cubed and held cold until needed

2 to 3 tablespoons ice water

FOR THE TART

¼ cup sugar

¼ cup dark brown sugar

½ teaspoon ground cinnamon

¼ teaspoon kosher salt

4 ripe plantains, yellow and black, halved lengthwise

2 tablespoons dark rum

3 tablespoons unsalted butter, melted, plus more for greasing

To make the crust, sift together the dry ingredients and pulse in a food processor to distribute evenly. Add the butter and pulse together until the butter flakes into pea-size pieces, 1 to 2 minutes. Gradually add the ice water and pulse until the dough just holds together.

Turn out the dough onto a lightly floured surface. For the final blending, smear the dough a few spoonfuls at a time with the heel of your hand. Gather the dough with a scraper and shape into a round disc. Wrap the dough in plastic wrap and refrigerate at least 1 hour or overnight.

Preheat the oven to 375°F. Grease a 9-inch pie plate or rectangular baking pan with butter.

Combine the sugars, cinnamon, and salt in a small bowl. Sprinkle the bottom of the greased pan evenly with half of the sugar mixture. Layer the plantains cut-side up in the pie plate. Drizzle the plantains with the rum and top with the remaining sugar mixture. Pour the melted butter over the plantains.

On a lightly floured surface, roll out the dough to a round, ⅛ inch thick. Dock the dough so that it rises evenly, using a fork to make small incisions. Lay the dough over the plantains, so that they are entirely covered and fold the corners back on themselves. Place in the preheated oven and bake until the crust is lightly browned, 45 to 60 minutes.

Remove the tart from the oven and unmold while still warm. Set a serving dish over the pie plate and carefully flip, allowing the caramel to drip down over the tart. Serve with a scoop of *Helado de Coco (page 275)* ice cream or whipped cream.

Cornmeal Cake with Coconut and Guava

PAN DE MAÍZ CON COCO Y GUAYABA

SERVES 6 TO 8

When Nereida Pardo offered to show me how to make this Pan de Maíz, *I expected a small cornmeal cake made with freshly shredded coconut and a few slices of guava. Though her children and grandchildren request it often, she hadn't made it in a while, so she decided to double and then triple the recipe. Extra cans of condensed and evaporated milk suddenly appeared and soon she was using her largest pot over two burners, and every surface in her Miami kitchen was covered with tins filled to the brim. Soon there wasn't a leftover crumb in the house.*

2 large frozen banana leaves, thawed

3 cups of water

2 cups freshly grated coconut

One 14-ounce can sweetened condensed milk

One 12-ounce can evaporated milk

4 tablespoons (½ stick) unsalted butter, cubed

2 teaspoons kosher salt

1½ cups fine cornmeal

½ cup black seedless raisins (optional)

4 ounces guava paste, cut into ½-inch-thick slices

SPECIAL EQUIPMENT:
One 10-inch springform pan

Preheat the oven to 350°F.

Wipe the banana leaves clean. Cut each leaf into 10 x 6-inch rectangles. Warm the leaves over a gas or electric burner over low heat by carefully passing each cut leaf over the burner, moving constantly until the leaves release their oils and become fragrant, 2 to 3 times. Line a 10-inch springform pan with banana leaves.

Combine the water, coconut, condensed milk, and evaporated milk in a blender, and pulse until well combined. Combine the coconut mixture, butter, and salt in a 6-quart heavy-bottomed pot. Bring to a simmer over medium heat and whisk in the cornmeal in a steady stream. Immediately lower the heat and continue to stir until the batter thickens slightly, 5 to 10 minutes. Stir in the raisins, if using.

Pour the cornmeal batter into the prepared pan and spread it evenly with a rubber spatula. Decorate the surface of the cake with the guava paste and cover with the remaining banana leaf.

Place the cake in the oven and bake until firm but still creamy, 20 to 30 minutes. Unmold and serve.

Cuban Layer Cake

CAKE CUBANO

SERVES 10 TO 12

Birdlike and energetic, my aunt Alicia Figueredo would beg her mother to let her help in the kitchen—whether it was chopping vegetables, stirring pots, or cracking eggs. It's a sentiment I understand because Tía Alicia is now my favorite person to spend time with in the kitchen. Like her mother before her, she lets me stay, so long as I stay busy. Working from the barely held-together cookbooks she brought with her from Cuba, she always brings elements of traditional Creole cooking to our family dinners, culminating in the classic celebration cake— rich cake layers of panetela *layered with* natilla *and covered in meringue.*

FOR THE *PANETELA*

2 cups unbleached all-purpose flour, plus more for dusting

1 tablespoon baking powder

1 teaspoon kosher salt

12 tablespoons (1½ sticks) unsalted butter, cubed and at room temperature, plus more for greasing

1¼ cups sugar

3 large eggs

1 cup whole milk

1 teaspoon pure vanilla extract

SPECIAL EQUIPMENT:

Two 9 x 2-inch round cake pans

FOR THE *NATILLA*

1¼ cups water

½ cup sugar

1 cup milk

4 large egg yolks

2½ tablespoons cornstarch

⅛ teaspoon kosher salt

1 teaspoon pure vanilla extract

FOR THE MERINGUE

2 large egg whites

1 cup sugar

⅓ cup water

⅛ teaspoon cream of tartar

Preheat the oven to 350°F. Butter two 9 x 2-inch round cake pans with butter and dust inside with flour, shaking out the excess. Set aside.

To prepare the panetela, sift together the flour, baking powder, and salt in a medium mixing bowl and set aside.

In a stand mixer fitted with the paddle attachment, beat the butter and sugar on medium speed until pale and fluffy, about 5 minutes. Add the eggs one at a time, beating for about 30 seconds after each addition.

In a small measuring cup, combine the milk and vanilla. On low speed or by hand, add the flour mixture to the sugar-and-butter mixture in three batches, alternating with the milk and ending with the flour. Do not overmix.

Pour the batter into the prepared cake pans. Set in the preheated oven and bake until lightly golden and a tester comes out clean, 30 to 35 minutes. Remove the cakes from the oven and allow to rest in the pans for 10 minutes. Run a thin knife around the edge of each cake pan and invert over a rack, then invert again so each cake is upright. Allow to cool completely before filling.

To prepare the pastry cream, combine the water and sugar in a saucepan and bring to a boil. Simmer over medium heat until it thickens slightly and registers 200°F on a candy thermometer, 5 to 10 minutes. Set aside to cool.

Combine the milk, egg yolks, cornstarch, and salt in a mixing bowl and whisk until the mixture is well combined and there are no visible yolks. Pass the milk mixture through a fine-mesh sieve into a separate 3- to 4-quart saucepan. Whisk in the cooled syrup and cook over medium-low heat, stirring constantly with a wooden spoon, until it thickens and coats the back of the spoon, 25 to 30 minutes. Remove the saucepan from the heat and stir in the vanilla. It will continue to thicken as it cools. If not using immediately, cover the surface of the cream with parchment paper and refrigerate until chilled, up to 2 days.

Prepare the meringue. Combine the sugar and water in a saucepan and bring to a boil. Simmer over medium heat until it reaches the thread stage and registers 230°F on a candy thermometer, 10 to 15 minutes.

In a stand mixer fitted with the whisk attachment, beat the egg whites on low speed until foamy, about a minute. Add the cream of tartar and increase the speed to medium until they hold soft peaks. Add the syrup, a little at a time, and beat on high speed until it forms stiff, glossy peaks.

To assemble the cake, place a cake layer on a plate or cake stand. Cover with the pastry cream and top with the remaining cake layer. Generously cover the cake with the meringue frosting.

Tomato Jam

DULCE DE TOMATE

MAKES 2 CUPS

Artist Claudia Paneca always wears black, but when I asked if she had any favorite family recipes, she went red with excitement describing her mother's Dulce de Tomate. *In this rustic jam, the tomatoes are quartered and simmered with sugar until the peels become candied and jewel-like. Served with fresh farmer cheese and Cuban crackers, it adds a little color to a monochromatic day.*

3 pounds ripe plum tomatoes, rinsed, trimmed, and quartered

1⅓ cups sugar

¼ cup lemon juice

Zest of one lemon

1 whole cinnamon stick

½ vanilla bean, split lengthwise (optional)

Combine the tomatoes, sugar, lemon juice, zest, cinnamon, and vanilla bean, if using, in a heavy 4-quart pot with a tight-fitting lid. Stir to combine and bring to a simmer over medium heat. Reduce the heat to medium-low and continue to cook, covered, checking frequently, until the tomatoes darken, the syrup thickens, and the peels become candied, 2 to 2¼ hours.

Remove the pot from the heat and allow to cool completely. Pour the jam into sterilized glass jars and seal.

Sweetened Coconut

DULCE DE COCO

MAKES 4 CUPS

Freshly grated coconut simmered with sugar and cinnamon is served on its own with cream cheese for a quick weekday dessert. It also makes a great filling for Pastelitos *(page 311),* Empanadas *(page 32), or* Casquitos de Guayaba *(page 266).*

4 cups fresh coconut (from 2 to 3 dried coconuts), finely shredded

4 cups sugar

1 whole cinnamon stick

Combine the shredded coconut and 8 cups of water in a heavy 4- to 5-quart pot. Bring to a boil over medium heat and simmer until tender, about 30 minutes. Stir in the sugar and cinnamon and continue to simmer until the syrup has thickened, 30 to 45 minutes. Remove from the heat and allow to cool. Pour into sterilized glass jars and seal.

NOTE

To use for fillings, allow the coconut to cook an additional 15 to 30 minutes until most of the syrup is absorbed. The sweetened coconut will continue to thicken as it cools.

Coconut and Almond Candy Cones

CUCURUCHOS DE COCO Y ALMENDRAS

MAKES 12 TO 16 *CUCURUCHOS*

Cucuruchos de Coco—*cones of freshly grated coconut cooked down with sugar, blended with fruits, nuts, and spices, and wrapped in palm leaves—are a specialty of Baracoa. This recipe comes from Maria Jiménez who makes them alongside her family using almonds from their own trees and fresh honey. The candied coconut can be wrapped in parchment paper cones or baked off* to make Coco Quemado *(see below).*

1½ cups raw whole almonds

4 cups fresh coconut (from 2 to 3 dried coconuts), finely shredded

1 cup sugar

1 cup mild honey

Preheat the oven to 350°F.

Spread the almonds on a baking sheet in a single layer. Place in the preheated oven and toast until fragrant, stirring frequently, 5 to 7 minutes. Remove the almonds and cool on a rack until ready to use.

Combine the shredded coconut and 6 cups of water in a heavy 4- to 5-quart pot. Bring to a boil over medium heat and simmer until the coconut is tender and most of the water has evaporated, about 30 minutes.

Stir in the sugar and honey and continue to simmer until the coconut is lightly golden and pulls away from sides of the pot, 25 to 30 minutes. Cool the candied coconut to room temperature.

To prepare the *cucuruchos*, using a roll of wax or parchment paper, cut out long triangles (about 15 x 14 x 6 inches). Position the triangle with the longest edge closest to you. Fold the right tip of the longest edge so that it meets the opposite corner. Roll into a funnel shape by wrapping the opposite end of the triangle around itself until it forms a cone. Tuck the tail end of the triangle into the top layer or secure with tape to seal.

Fill each cone with 3 to 4 tablespoons of candied coconut. Fold the tips of the cones down over the coconut to close. Serve on its own or as a topping for ice cream.

Variation: COCO QUEMADO | CRISPY COCONUT COOKIES
MAKES 24 COOKIES

Preheat the oven to 350°F. Line a 13 x 18 x 1-inch baking sheet with parchment paper or a nonstick liner. Mound spoonfuls of candied coconut onto the prepared baking sheet. Place in the preheated oven and bake until browned and crispy, 10 minutes. Cool in the baking sheet until firm, about 10 more minutes, before transferring to a rack.

Poached Guava Shells

CASQUITOS DE GUAYABA

SERVES 8

Floating in a lightly spiced syrup, Casquitos de Guayaba *are seemingly tender. But Getrudis Rodríguez taught me that the only way to achieve that delicate balance is to put them through a hard simmer.*

2 pounds whole guavas, preferably red, rinsed and trimmed

2 cups sugar

1 whole cinnamon stick

1 teaspoon whole allspice berries (optional)

Lime zest

Peel the guavas, slice in half, and scoop out all the pulp and seeds (see note). Place the guava shells in a heavy 4- to 5-quart pot with 6 cups of water to cover. Simmer over medium-low heat until tender, 20 to 30 minutes. Strain the guava shells and reserve 4 cups of the cooking water.

Combine the reserved cooking water, sugar, cinnamon stick, and allspice, if using, in the same pot. Add the guava shells back to the pot and bring to a simmer over medium-high heat. Keep at a fast simmer until the liquid has the consistency of a light syrup, 30 to 45 minutes. Set aside to cool then pour the syrup and the shells into sterilized jars and refrigerate. Serve cold or at room temperature with cream cheese and crackers.

Variation: GUAYABAS RELLENAS | STUFFED GUAVAS

Prepare the guava shells as directed. Remove from the syrup when tender and place in a baking dish. Fill each guava shell with 2 tablespoons of *Dulce de Coco (page 262)* and chill, at least 30 minutes. Drizzle with syrup and serve.

NOTE

The pulp and seeds can be used for making *Guava Marmalade (page 27)*. If not using immediately, refrigerate for one week or freeze for up to three months.

Cuban Vanilla Ice Cream

MANTECADO

MAKES 1 QUART

While the lineup at the ¡Azucar! Ice Cream Company *always includes classic Cuban ice-cream flavors such as guava, mamey, and coconut, Suzy Battle received endless requests for* mantecado—*a rich vanilla ice cream she'd only ever heard about. Suzy invited the domino players permanently perched across the street from her Little Havana shop to test the recipe until she got it right. She generously shared the results with me adapted for small homemade batches.*

FOR THE CUSTARD

6 large egg yolks

1 cup whole milk

1 cup sugar

1½ teaspoons unbleached all-purpose flour

¼ teaspoon kosher salt

Pinch ground cinnamon

Pinch ground nutmeg

2 teaspoons pure vanilla extract

3 large egg whites, at room temperature

5 tablespoons sugar

One 12-ounce can evaporated milk, chilled

To prepare the custard, combine the egg yolks, whole milk, 1 cup sugar, flour, salt, cinnamon, and nutmeg in a food processor or blender and pulse until well blended. Pass the milk mixture through a fine-mesh sieve into a 3- to 4-quart saucepan. Cook over medium heat, stirring constantly, until the custard covers the back of a wooden spoon, 4 to 6 minutes. Remove the saucepan from the heat and stir in the vanilla extract. Chill the custard at least 2 hours or overnight.

In a stand mixer fitted with the whisk attachment, beat the egg whites on low speed until foamy, about 1 minute. Gradually add the remaining 5 tablespoons sugar and beat on medium speed until it forms stiff peaks, about 5 minutes. Add the chilled evaporated milk and continue to beat until it thickens slightly, 2 to 3 additional minutes. Stir in the prepared custard and mix until well blended. Process in an ice-cream maker according to manufacturer's instructions, 15 to 20 minutes. Freeze until ready to serve.

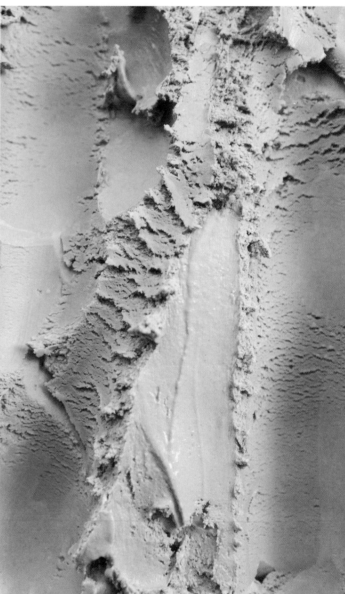

ON A BRIGHT CORNER OF LITTLE HAVANA, parents herd their children past an enormous painting of Cuban icon Celia Cruz into the *¡Azucar! Ice Cream Company*. Settling into the guayabera-lined benches with their feet barely touching the floor's colorful Cuban tiles, the children dip into flan ice cream drizzled with *caramelo* syrup or a refreshing *guarapiña* sorbet made with sugarcane and pineapple juice, and watch the sun-dazed tourists drift between the ongoing domino games, *ventanitas*, and cigar shops that line *Calle Ocho*. Though born and raised in Miami, Suzy Battle was new to the neighborhood when she left behind a career in finance to open *¡Azucar!*. The inspiration came from her grandmother. Born in Cuba and married to a sugar mill engineer, Isabel de la Torre traveled throughout Central and South America, making ice cream with the new fruits she discovered along the way and compiling the detailed notebooks Battle still consults. As a result, Battle can't point to just one recipe that comes from her grandmother. "The whole store is hers," explains Battle.

HELADOS DE FRUTA:
CHIRIMOYA, COCO, FRESA, Y MAMEY

MAKES 1 QUART

Fruit didn't last very long in our family's home in La Víbora. My great-aunt Ninita would bring home a bag of scaly cherimoyas or ripe mameys and they would disappear—only to turn up in one of her sister Amelia's still lifes a few weeks later. Occasionally she turned them into ice cream, too. Each sister had their favorite recipe and everyone who came through the house while it was being made took a turn at the hand-crank machine. Looking through an old family cookbook, I found Amelia's cherimoya and mamey, Elena's coconut, and Sofía's strawberry recipes, which I've adapted here.

HELADO DE CHIRIMOYA | CHIRIMOYA ICE CREAM

4 cups cherimoya pulp, fresh or frozen (see note)

¾ cup whole milk

¾ cup sugar

1 tablespoon light rum

One 12-ounce can evaporated milk, chilled

Combine the cherimoya pulp, milk, sugar, and rum in a blender or food processor and pulse until well combined. Chill the cherimoya mixture at least 2 hours or overnight. In a stand mixer fitted with the whisk attachment, beat the chilled evaporated milk at medium speed and until it thickens slightly, 2 to 3 minutes. Stir in the cherimoya mixture and mix until well blended. Process in an ice-cream maker according to the manufacturer's instructions, 15 to 20 minutes. Freeze until ready to serve.

HELADO DE COCO | COCONUT ICE CREAM

MAKES 1 QUART

2 cups whole milk

1½ cups sugar

2 tablespoons cornstarch

2 cups fresh Coconut Milk (page 298), 2 cups best-quality canned unsweetened coconut milk

1 tablespoon light rum

Whisk together the whole milk, sugar, and cornstarch in a small saucepan until well combined. Bring to a simmer over medium heat, stirring constantly, until slightly thickened, 5 to 7 minutes. Remove the saucepan from the heat and stir in the coconut milk and rum. Cool to room temperature and chill at least 2 hours or overnight. Process in an ice-cream maker according to the manufacturer's instructions, 15 to 20 minutes. Freeze until ready to serve.

HELADO DE FRESA | STRAWBERRY ICE CREAM
MAKES 1 QUART

2 pounds fresh strawberries, rinsed, hulled, and halved

1 cup sugar

1 tablespoon freshly squeezed lemon juice

1 tablespoon light rum

1 cup whole milk

2 tablespoons cornstarch

One 12-ounce can evaporated milk, chilled

Place the strawberries in a bowl and toss with sugar, lemon juice, and rum. Allow to macerate at room temperature, at least 1 hour or overnight.

In the meantime, whisk together the whole milk and cornstarch in a small saucepan until well combined. Bring to a simmer over medium heat, stirring constantly, until slightly thickened, 3 to 5 minutes. Cool to room temperature.

Place the macerated strawberries in a blender or food processor and pulse until smooth. Strain the strawberry mixture into the cooled milk mixture and chill at least 2 hours or overnight.

In a stand mixer fitted with the whisk attachment, beat the chilled evaporated milk until it thickens slightly, 2 to 3 minutes. Stir in the strawberry-milk mixture and mix until well blended. Process in an ice-cream maker according to the manufacturer's instructions, 15 to 20 minutes. Freeze until ready to serve.

HELADO DE MAMEY COLORADO | RED MAMEY ICE CREAM

MAKES 1 QUART

1½ cups water

1 cup sugar

1 tablespoon freshly squeezed lime juice

4 cups mamey pulp, fresh or frozen (see note)

½ cup whole milk

1 tablespoon light rum

Combine the water and sugar in a small saucepan and bring to a boil. Simmer until it reaches a honeylike consistency and registers 230°F on a candy thermometer, about 20 minutes. Cool the syrup to room temperature.

Combine the cooled syrup, mamey, milk, and rum in a blender and pulse until well combined. Chill the mamey mixture at least 2 hours or overnight. Process in an ice-cream maker according to the manufacturer's instructions, 15 to 20 minutes. Freeze until ready to serve.

NOTE

Tropical fruit purées can be purchased frozen in Latin American markets. If using fresh fruit, peel and seed the fruit, then roughly chop. Place the chopped fruit in a blender or food processor and pulse until it forms a smooth purée. Strain the purée and discard the solids. Use immediately or freeze and store for later use, up to 6 months. Defrost in the refrigerator before using and proceed with the recipe as directed.

BAKED CHOCOLATE ICE CREAM "EL CARMELO"

SERVES 8

This dessert was a favorite at El Carmelo, a popular Havana café. Similar to a baked Alaska, chocolate ice cream is topped with meringue then set under a broiler until the peaks are browned. It always reminds me of my grandmother's lunch group who often served it at their get-togethers. Silvery women with smoky voices wrapped in a cloud of Chanel No. 5 and Aqua Net, they called themselves las cucharitas *since every meal ended with a single dessert and lots of "little spoons." Any good-quality chocolate ice cream will work, but I enjoy it with* Chocolate Rum Ice Cream *(page 280).*

FOR THE CRUST

30 galletas Maria crackers (about 2 cups), ground to crumbs

6 tablespoons (¾ stick) unsalted butter, melted

FOR THE FILLING

1 quart Chocolate Rum Ice Cream (page 280) or best-quality chocolate ice cream

FOR THE MERINGUE

4 large egg whites

Pinch cream of tartar

¾ cup sugar

½ teaspoon pure vanilla extract

Prepare the crust. Preheat the oven to 350°F. Grease a 9-inch square baking pan with nonstick cooking spray.

In a large mixing bowl, combine the cookie crumbs and melted butter until the mixture holds together. Fill the prepared pan with the crumb mixture and press into the bottom and sides of the pan to form an even crust. Bake in the preheated oven until lightly browned, 10 to 12 minutes. Remove the pan from the oven and set aside to cool completely. Freeze until ready to use.

Scoop the chocolate ice cream into the prepared crust, smoothing the top with an offset spatula (this works best if the ice cream is thawed a few minutes beforehand). Return to the freezer until firm, at least 30 minutes.

To prepare the meringue, in a stand mixer fitted with the whisk attachment, beat the egg whites on low speed until foamy, about 1 minute. Add the cream of tartar and increase the speed to medium until they hold soft peaks. Gradually add the sugar followed by vanilla extract and beat on high speed until it forms stiff, glossy peaks, about 5 more minutes. Cover the pie with the meringue and return to the freezer until ready to serve.

To serve, preheat the broiler. Set the pie under the broiler until lightly toasted. It should take no more than 1 to 2 minutes and should be watched closely. Serve immediately.

CHOCOLATE RUM ICE CREAM
MAKES 1 QUART

5 ounces high-quality bittersweet chocolate (70% cocoa), finely chopped

2 ounces brewed espresso

6 large egg yolks

¾ cup sugar

1½ cups whole milk

One 12-ounce can evaporated milk

1 tablespoon dark rum

Place the chocolate and freshly brewed espresso in a double boiler or small heatproof bowl set over a pot of gently simmering water. Stir with a small spoon or rubber spatula until the chocolate melts, 3 to 5 minutes. Set aside.

In a stand mixer fitted with the whisk attachment, beat together the egg yolks and sugar until they are pale and form a ribbon, about 5 minutes.

Place the milk and evaporated milk in a medium saucepan and bring to a simmer over medium heat. Carefully add 1 cup of the heated milk to the egg yolks to temper the eggs then add this mixture to the saucepan.

Whisk in the melted chocolate until well combined. Simmer the custard over low heat, stirring constantly until it thickens and coats the back of the spoon, about 5 minutes. Remove from the heat and strain into a clean mixing bowl. Stir in the rum. Cool completely then cover with plastic wrap and chill at least 2 hours or overnight.

Process in an ice-cream maker according to the manufacturer's instructions, 15 to 20 minutes. Freeze until ready to use.

CHOROTE CON CHURROS

SERVES 6 TO 8

Cultivated in Baracoa since the seventeenth century, fermented cacao beans are traditionally ground into a paste and shaped into a ball with just enough flour to hold it together. Raised on her mother's small cacao farm, Esperanza still makes hers by hand, preferring the darkest possible chocolate that retains the entire soul of the cacao. In this typical preparation for Chorote *she gave me, which I've adapted here, dark chocolate is blended with spiced coconut milk and thickened with corn starch.*

FOR THE *CHOROTE*

4 cups fresh Coconut Milk (page 298) or best-quality canned unsweetened coconut milk or whole milk

1 whole cinnamon stick

1 tablespoon whole allspice berries

1 teaspoon whole cloves

1 tablespoon cornstarch

7 ounces high-quality bittersweet chocolate (70% cocoa), chopped

FOR THE CHURROS

2 cups water

6 tablespoons (¾ stick) unsalted butter

1 teaspoon pure vanilla extract

1 teaspoon kosher salt

2 cups unbleached all-purpose flour

4 cups canola oil for frying

1 cup sugar

1 tablespoon ground cinnamon

Pinch ground clove (optional)

SPECIAL EQUIPMENT:

Metal or plastic *churrera* (churro maker) or pastry bag fitted with ½-inch star tip

To make the *chorote*, combine the milk, cinnamon, allspice, and cloves in a medium saucepan and bring to a simmer over medium heat, about 10 minutes. Whisk in the cornstarch until well combined. Whisk in the chocolate and return to a simmer, stirring constantly, until it is completely melted and smooth, 5 to 7 minutes. Strain the chocolate mixture and discard the solids.

To make the churros, combine the water, butter, vanilla, and salt in a medium saucepan and bring to a boil. Lower the heat to medium-low and slowly beat in the flour with a wooden spoon until the dough is smooth, 2 to 3 minutes. Allow the dough mixture to cool for 1 to 2 minutes.

Heat the oil over medium-high heat in a heavy 3- to 4-quart pot to 375°F.

Transfer the dough to a *churrera* or pastry bag fitted with a star tip. Working in batches, pipe a 6-inch strip of dough directly into the oil and fry, turning once, until

lightly golden on all sides, 2 to 3 minutes total. Transfer the churros to a plate lined with paper towels to drain. Repeat with the remaining dough.

Combine the sugar, cinnamon, and clove, if using, in a large shallow bowl. Roll the churros in the sugar mixture while they are still warm and set them on a platter. Serve with the *chorote*.

NOTE

Churros can be piped onto a baking sheet lined with wax paper before transferring to the oil. They can also be made in advance and chilled up to 2 hours before frying.

COCKTAILS

Catalan merchant Don Facundo Bacardi Massó and French Cuban José León Bouteiller did not invent Cuban rum in their small wood-plank distillery in Santiago de Cuba, in 1862, but they may have made it drinkable. The exact recipe they hit on to produce their distinctively light and mild rum is a well-kept secret, but many credit their application of charcoal filtration to remove impurities and the use of American white oak barrels for aging. Sold in Magín Bacardi's general store, their rum was soon given a name, while the bats drawn to the molasses they used in the distillation process gave it a symbol. Once the rum started flowing, many more jumped in. The history of Cuban rum is told through distillers, drinkers, and most important, *cantineros*—barmen whose first names are forever attached to the bright cocktails and concoctions they helped create.

CUBA LIBRE | *rum and coke* . . . 289

EL PRESIDENTE . . . 289

MOJITO . . . 290

DAIQUIRÍ . . . 294

CREMA DE VIE | *cuban egg nog* . . . 295

Rum and Coke

CUBA LIBRE

SERVES 1

While the slogan dates from Cuba's War of Independence, the origin of the Cuba Libre cocktail is less clear. Many credit it to Barrio, a Havana barman who kept plenty of Coca-Cola on hand to serve the U.S. military personnel who patronized his bar. Eventually, he threw in some rum and a battle cry became a celebratory toast.

2 ounces white rum
Coca-Cola to top off

1 slice lime

Pour rum in a tall 8-ounce glass. Fill with ice cubes and top off with Coca-Cola and a slice of lime.

EL PRESIDENTE

SERVES 1

A popular cocktail in the 1920s, many claim it was named after Gerardo Machado, Cuba's President during Prohibition. I asked his granddaughter Nena Santeiro for the recipe, but she couldn't imagine why the cocktail had been named for her grandfather who she'd never known to touch a drop.

2 ounces white rum
1 ounce dry French vermouth

Dash of best-quality grenadine syrup
Slice of orange rind

Combine vermouth and rum in a mixing glass filled with ice. Stir, strain, and serve in a chilled glass. Add a dash of grenadine to taste. Garnish with orange rind.

MOJITO

SERVES 1

Though Hemingway popularized the drink with a single backhanded compliment to his favorite Havana watering holes, declaring, "My mojito in La Bodeguita, my daiquirí in El Floridita," the cocktail's origin can be traced back to the sixteenth-century el Draque, a crude blend of lime, sugar and aguardiente, invented by pirates on expedition with Sir Francis Drake. Eventually, the aguardiente was replaced with smooth, light-bodied rums elaborated in the late 1800s and the Mojito—an African word roughly translated as "little spell"—was cast. This recipe comes from my uncle Guillermo Tremols who learned it from Deus, a bartender at Havana's Miramar Yacht Club.

12 fresh spearmint leaves with stems

1 ounce freshly squeezed lime juice

1½ tablespoons confectioners' sugar

2½ ounces white rum

2 to 3 ounces club soda, to top off

1 to 2 dashes Angostura bitters (optional)

Muddle the mint, lime juice, and sugar in an 8-ounce glass until the mint is gently bruised. Stir in the rum and add ice. Top off with club soda. Add Angostura bitters, if using, to taste. Garnish with a sprig of mint.

VICTOR'S CAFÉ IN NEW YORK'S THEATER District has been the unofficial Cuban embassy for years. Arriving in Manhattan from Guanabacoa in 1957, Victor del Corral and his wife, Eloina, couldn't have imagined the wave of exiles from Cuba who would follow them a few short years later. When they did come, the couple gave whatever they could—whether it was a room, a meal, or a job. Working in restaurant kitchens throughout the city, Victor eventually saved enough money to open the first Victor's Café on Columbus Avenue in 1963. "Whoever came to Victor's was coming to his house, the restaurant was our living room," says his daughter Sonia Zaldívar. Many of their earliest recipes came from Eloina, who was always cooking for anyone who turned up while Victor just loved being around people. The restaurant is now run by Victor's children and grandchildren, the third generation to call the café home.

DAIQUIRÍ

SERVES 1

This drink is named for the Daiquirí mines where American Jennings Cox was a general manager. Cox is credited with using the gallon allotment of Bacardi rum he was partially paid with and blending it with sugar, lime juice, and ice. Immortalized in Hemingway's Islands in the Stream, *Constantino "Constante" Ribalaigua Vert made the cocktail famous at Havana's El Floridita. Asked by British travel writer Basil Woon why he didn't seek his fortune in Paris, he replied, "I no do so badly here." The* cantineros *in Havana's El Chanchullero just off the Plaza de Cristo carry on the tradition. They kindly made me a daiquirí in stop motion, pausing just long enough for me to count the spoonfuls of sugar added and number of key limes used.*

2 ounces white rum

1½ tablespoons sugar

1 ounce fresh key lime juice

1 teaspoon Maraschino liqueur

Combine all ingredients in a cocktail shaker filled with ice. Shake, strain, and serve in a chilled glass.

Variation: DAIQUIRÍ FRAPPÉ

Combine all ingredients in a blender with 2 cups of ice and pulse on high speed until frothy. Serve in a chilled glass.

Cuban Egg Nog

CREMA DE VIE

MAKES 6 CUPS

Rich with egg yolks and sweetened with syrup, every family has their own Crema de Vie *recipe they bottle at Christmastime for gifts and parties and this is ours.*

FOR THE SYRUP

1 cup water

1½ cups sugar

One 14-ounce can sweetened
    condensed milk

One 12-ounce can evaporated milk

4 large egg yolks

1½ cups white rum

1 teaspoon pure vanilla extract

Pinch of kosher salt

Ground cinnamon

Freshly ground nutmeg

Combine the water and sugar in a saucepan and bring to a boil. Simmer over medium heat until it thickens slightly and registers 230°F on a candy thermometer, 15 to 20 minutes. Set aside to cool.

    Combine the condensed milk, evaporated milk, egg yolks, rum, vanilla, salt, cinnamon and nutmeg to taste in a blender and pulse until well blended. Pour in the cooled syrup and blend on high speed until frothy. Keep chilled until ready to serve.

FOUNDATION RECIPES

ACHIOTE OIL . . . 298

COCONUT MILK . . . 298

PAN DE MANTECA . . . 299

PAN DE AGUA . . . 299

PAN DE MEDIA NOCHE . . . 300

MOJO CRIOLLO | *creole garlic sauce* . . . 301

PURÉ DE TOMATE | *tomato purée* . . . 304

SOFRITO . . . 305

BEEF STOCK . . . 306

CHICKEN STOCK . . . 306

FISH STOCK . . . 307

ACHIOTE OIL

MAKES 1 CUP

Well-sealed, achiote oil will keep in the refrigerator for up to 1 month.

1 cup extra-virgin olive or canola oil

½ cup achiote seeds (also known as *annatto*)

Combine the achiote seeds and oil in a small saucepan and bring to a simmer over low heat, about 5 minutes. Remove from the heat and allow the seeds to steep until the oil turns a deep red color, about 10 additional minutes. Set aside to cool. Strain the oil and discard the seeds. Pour into a glass jar and seal.

COCONUT MILK

MAKES 2 CUPS

2 large whole dried coconuts

2 cups warm water

Preheat the oven to 400°F.

Open the holes in the coconut's "eyes" with a corkscrew. Invert the coconut over a bowl or measuring cup and drain. Reserve the coconut water for another use.

Place the coconuts in the oven for about 15 minutes. Set each coconut over a dish towel then tap with a hammer until it cracks open. Scoop out the coconut meat from the hard outer shell using a spoon. Peel the brown outer layer and chop it into small cubes, about 4 cups.

Place a fine-mesh sieve lined with tightly woven cheesecloth over a mixing bowl and set aside. Working in batches, combine 2 cups of cubed coconut and 1 cup of warm water in a blender. Pulse on high speed until the coconut is finely shredded, about 30 seconds at a time. Pass the coconut through the prepared sieve then wring out the coconut using the cheesecloth to extract as much liquid as possible. Repeat with the remaining coconut and water until you have 2 cups of extracted coconut milk. Discard the solids.

PAN DE MANTECA

MAKES 3 LARGE LOAVES OR 12 SMALL ROLLS

1½ cups warm water (110°F to 115°F)

1 tablespoon active dry yeast

1 tablespoon sugar

4 tablespoons best-quality lard, at room temperature

1 tablespoon kosher salt

4 cups unbleached all-purpose flour, divided

Canola or olive oil for greasing

1 frozen plantain leaf, defrosted and sliced into 6-inch strips

SPECIAL EQUIPMENT: Baking stone

Combine the yeast, sugar, and water in the bowl of a stand mixer. Let it stand until it begins to foam, about 10 minutes.

Using the paddle attachment, mix in the lard and salt on low speed until well incorporated, 1 to 2 minutes.

Switch to the dough hook attachment and slowly add 3½ cups of flour and mix on low speed until the dough begins to pull away from the sides of the bowl. Increase the speed to medium and continue to knead until the dough is smooth but still sticky, 8 to 10 minutes.

Lightly oil a large mixing bowl. Shape the dough into a ball and place in the greased bowl turning over once. Cover the bowl with lightly oiled plastic wrap and place in a warm, draft-free place. Allow to rise until it doubles in bulk, 1 to 1½ hours.

Place a baking stone in the center rack of the oven and preheat the oven to 400°F. Line a 13 x 18 x 1-inch baking sheet with parchment paper or a nonstick liner.

Turn the dough out onto a lightly floured surface. Divide the dough into 3 equal pieces. Using a rolling pin, roll out the first piece to a rectangle, 6 by 12 inches. Sprinkle lightly with remaining flour then fold the dough in half lengthwise and roll out again. Roll the dough into a baguette-shaped loaf. At this point, the loaf can also be divided into 4 equal pieces and shaped into individual rolls. Repeat with the remaining dough. Place the loaves seam-side down on the prepared baking sheet.

Score each piece of dough down the middle with a sharp knife and tuck a strip of plantain leaf into the open seam lengthwise. Loosely cover the loaves with plastic wrap. Place the loaves in a warm, draft-free place and allow to rest, about 30 minutes.

Place each loaf directly on top of the baking stone and bake until lightly golden and hollow sounding when tapped, 25 to 30 minutes (for loaves) and 20 to 25 minutes (for rolls).

Variation: **PAN DE AGUA**

Airy and pale *pan de agua* works best for pressed Cuban sandwiches. Simply omit the lard and proceed with the recipe as directed.

PAN DE MEDIA NOCHE

MAKES 8 LARGE ROLLS OR 16 SMALL ROLLS

¾ cup warm water (110°F to 115°F)

¾ cup warm milk (110°F to 115°F)

½ cup sugar

1 tablespoon active dry yeast

3 large eggs, well-beaten

2 tablespoons mild honey

2½ cups unbleached all-purpose flour

2½ cups unbleached bread flour

2 teaspoons kosher salt

8 tablespoons (1 stick) unsalted butter, melted and cooled to room temperature, plus more to glaze rolls

1 egg beaten with 1 tablespoon water

Combine the water, milk, sugar, and yeast in the bowl of a stand mixer. Let it stand until it begins to foam, about 10 minutes.

Using the paddle attachment, add the eggs and honey to the yeast mixture and stir at low speed until well incorporated, 1 to 2 minutes.

Combine the all-purpose flour, bread flour, and salt in a large mixing bowl. Switch to the dough hook attachment and add the flour mixture, one cup at a time, alternating with the melted butter, until both are well incorporated, 3 to 5 minutes.

Increase the speed to medium and continue to beat until the dough is smooth and elastic and pulls away from the sides of the bowl, 8 to 10 minutes. Pour the dough onto a lightly floured surface and shape into a ball.

Lightly oil a large mixing bowl. Place the dough in the greased bowl, punch it down, reshape it into a ball, and turn it over once. Cover the bowl with lightly oiled plastic wrap and place in a warm, draft-free place. Allow to rise until it doubles in bulk, 1 to 1½ hours.

Punch the dough down again and refrigerate the dough at least four hours or overnight.

The following day, bring the dough to room temperature, about 30 minutes.

Preheat the oven to 350°F. Line a 13 x 18 x 1-inch baking sheet with parchment paper or a nonstick liner.

Turn the dough out onto a lightly floured surface. Divide the dough into 8 equal pieces if making large rolls or 16 equal pieces if making small rolls. Shape each piece into a roll with slightly tapered ends. Transfer the rolls to the prepared baking sheet.

Brush the tops of the rolls with the egg wash. Bake until golden brown, about 30 to 35 minutes (for large) or about 25 to 30 minutes (for small). Remove the rolls from the oven, take them off the baking sheet, and let them cool on a wire rack. Brush the tops with additional melted butter while they are still warm.

Creole Garlic Sauce

MOJO CRIOLLO

MAKES 1 CUP

6 large garlic cloves, peeled and mashed

1 teaspoon kosher salt

½ teaspoon freshly ground black pepper

½ cup freshly squeezed sour orange juice or equal parts lime and orange juice

2 tablespoons fresh oregano, thinly chopped

½ cup best-quality lard or olive oil

Using a mortar and pestle, mash the garlic, salt, and black pepper to form a smooth paste. Whisk in the sour orange juice and oregano until well combined. Place the sour orange mixture in a medium saucepan with a tight-fitting lid.

Place the lard or olive oil in a separate small saucepan and bring to a simmer over medium heat.

Remove the cover of the saucepan away from your body and only enough to safely pour the lard or olive oil inside in one motion then replace the cover immediately. This should be done carefully because the liquid will bubble and spurt. Leave covered until the popping sound subsides, 3 to 5 minutes. This sauce does not keep well and should be used immediately.

Tomato Purée

PURÉ DE TOMATE

MAKES 4 CUPS

Though canned tomato purée is a pantry staple, making it at home is a great way to take advantage of abundant summer tomatoes and add in your own blend of spices. This recipe is adapted from Delicias de la Mesa—Manual de Cocina y Repostería *(1925) by María Antonieta Reyes Gavilán y Moenck.*

4 pounds ripe plum tomatoes

1 tablespoon sugar

1 tablespoon kosher or sea salt

1 teaspoon ground ginger

½ teaspoon ground cinnamon

½ teaspoon ground mustard

½ teaspoon ground nutmeg

2 tablespoons extra-virgin olive oil

Fill a large mixing bowl with ice water and set aside.

Bring a large pot of boiling water to a fast simmer. Score the bottom of each tomato with an X and trim the stem end. Working in batches, blanche the tomatoes in the boiling water and remove when the peels begin to pull away, less than a minute. Immediately remove the tomatoes with a slotted spoon and transfer to the ice water. Repeat with the remaining tomatoes.

When the tomatoes are cool enough to handle, peel the tomatoes and discard the skins. Combine the peeled tomatoes, sugar, salt, and spices in a blender or food processor and pulse until smooth. Strain the purée through a fine-mesh sieve, discarding the solids.

Simmer the purée in a large heavy pot over medium heat until slightly thickened, 10 to 15 minutes. Adjust the seasoning to taste. Allow to cool completely and pour into sterilized glass jars. Cover with olive oil and seal.

SOFRITO

MAKES 1 CUP

Cuban seasoning relies heavily on the trinity of green bell peppers, onion, and garlic, which can also be made in advance.

4 large green bell peppers, stemmed, cored, seeded, and cubed

4 large yellow onions, cubed

1 head of garlic, peeled

1 tablespoon kosher salt

1½ teaspoons freshly ground black pepper

½ cup extra-virgin olive oil

Combine all the ingredients in a food processor or blender and pulse to form a textured purée. When ready to use, sauté the *sofrito* in olive oil and proceed with the recipe as directed. The *sofrito* can be kept in a well-sealed container for up to five days.

STOCKS: BEEF, CHICKEN, AND FISH

BEEF STOCK

MAKES 6 CUPS

2 pounds flank steak or brisket, cut into 4 pieces

1 large yellow onion, quartered

1 large carrot, peeled and cut into 1-inch chunks

½ small red cabbage, quartered

½ small bunch fresh flat-leaf parsley, trimmed

2 sprigs fresh spearmint (optional)

4 large garlic cloves, peeled and crushed

1 teaspoon kosher salt

1 teaspoon whole black peppercorns

1 teaspoon whole allspice berries

½ teaspoon whole cloves

2 dried bay leaves

Line a fine-mesh sieve with a double thickness of cheesecloth. Freeze the lined strainer until ready to use.

Combine all the ingredients in a heavy 6-quart pot with 8 cups of water. Bring to a boil then reduce the heat to maintain a low simmer and cook covered until the beef is tender, 1½ to 2 hours. If the beef is not being used immediately, allow the beef to cool in the broth, then remove, and reserve for later use.

Pass the stock through the chilled sieve into a large mixing bowl. Discard the solids. Set aside to cool then refrigerate or freeze until needed.

CHICKEN STOCK

MAKES 6 CUPS

1 whole bone-in, skin-on chicken breast, halved

4 large plum tomatoes, quartered

1 large carrot, peeled and halved crosswise

1 large green bell pepper, stemmed, cored, seeded, and quartered

1 medium yellow onion, quartered

1 small bunch fresh flat-leaf parsley, trimmed

4 sprigs fresh oregano

4 garlic cloves, peeled and mashed

1 dried bay leaf

1 teaspoon kosher salt

1 teaspoon whole black peppercorns

½ teaspoon whole cumin seeds, crushed

Line a fine-mesh sieve with a double thickness of cheesecloth. Freeze the lined strainer until ready to use.

Combine all the ingredients in a 6-quart heavy pot with 8 cups of water. Bring to a steady simmer over medium heat, and cook, covered, for 20 to 25 minutes. If the chicken is not being used immediately, allow the chicken to cool in the broth, then remove, and reserve for later use.

Pass the stock through the chilled sieve into a large mixing bowl. Discard the solids. Set aside to cool then refrigerate or freeze until needed.

FISH STOCK

MAKES 6 CUPS

1 large fish head, grouper or snapper, cleaned and well-rinsed

4 plum tomatoes, quartered

1 bunch fresh flat-leaf parsley, trimmed

1 medium yellow onion, quartered

1 large cubanelle or green bell pepper, stemmed, cored, seeded, and quartered

1 tablespoon sea salt

1 teaspoon whole mixed peppercorns

Line a fine-mesh sieve with a double thickness of cheesecloth. Freeze the lined strainer until ready to use.

Combine all the ingredients and 8 cups of water in a 6-quart heavy pot or deep sauce-pan. Bring to a boil then lower the heat to medium-low, for 45 to 60 minutes. Pass the stock through the chilled sieve into a large mixing bowl. Discard the solids. Set aside to cool then refrigerate or freeze until needed.

NOTE

The stocks can be made in advance then kept refrigerated for 3 to 5 days or frozen for up to 2 months. If using frozen stock, defrost in the refrigerator and proceed as directed.

CUBAN PANTRY AND GLOSSARY

Here is an A to Z glossary of basic Cuban ingredients, cooking techniques and terms, appliances and gadgets.

A CABALLO
This term is used to describe a dish that has been finished with a fried egg on top.

ACHIOTE | ANNATTO
A small red seed grown throughout the island and used as a natural coloring agent. The seeds can be ground to a powder and used as a seasoning or heated in oil or liquid to extract its flavor and color then strained out. Also known as *annatto*, it is often used as a substitute for the more expensive saffron.

AJÍ | BELL PEPPER
Though a generic term for all peppers, this usually refers to green, red, or yellow bell peppers. They are often substituted with cubanelle (or Italian frying pepper). Together with onion and garlic, sweet peppers are part of the Cuban trinity that forms the base of every sofrito.

AJÍ CACHUCHA | CACHUCHA PEPPER
These small lantern-shaped peppers, also known as ají dulce, are used in sofritos and marinades. Typically sold green, they turn orange or red as they ripen on the vine. Mild and sweet, they should not to be confused with hot rocatillo, habanero, or Scotch bonnet peppers.

AJÍ GUAGUAO
Also known as ají picante, these fiery peppers are bright red and grow 1 to 2 inches long. Difficult to find in the United States, they can be substituted with tabasco, cayenne, habanero, or Scotch bonnet peppers.

ALCAPARRAS | CAPERS
The edible flower bud of the *Capparis spinosa* plant, which is salted and pickled, they are often used in "alcaparrado" dishes and blended with olives and raisins for a sweet-and-sour taste.

ALMÍBAR | SIMPLE SUGAR SYRUP
A mixture of water and sugar used to make meringues, soak cakes, or poach fruits.

ANNÓN | CUSTARD APPLE
A sweet tropical fruit with a custardlike white flesh under its green skin. Similar to cherimoyas and guanábana, it's eaten fresh or pulped and used in juices, shakes, and ice creams.

ARROZ | RICE
Long-grain or converted rice is preferred when the rice is served on the side or cooked with beans. The rice can be left unrinsed to retain the nutrients, or rinsed to remove the starch and make it fluffier when cooked.

Short-grain Valencia-style rice, which absorbs more liquid while retaining a creamy but al dente texture, is preferred when preparing paella-style dishes such as arroz con pollo. Arborio or Carnaroli rice can be substituted.

AZAFRÁN | SAFFRON
The crimson stigma of the crocus flower used for adding deep yellow and orange color. Introduced to Cuba via Spain, it imparts a slightly bitter but floral flavor to foods and rice dishes in particular.

BACALAO | SALT COD

Cod fish that has been salt cured to extract moisture and preserve the fish for long periods of time. It must be soaked and rinsed in several changes of cold water to remove the salt before consumption.

BAÑO MARÍA

Bain-Marie, or water baths, are used when cooking delicate custards in the oven.

BIJOL

This popular condiment containing achiote, corn flour, cumin, and coloring agents was created by Rafael Martínez in 1922 and is often substituted for the more expensive saffron.

BONIATO

A root vegetable also known as *batata* or *camote*, there are many varieties though white-flesh boniatos are preferable. Boniatos should be firm, free of any mold, and heavy for their size. They oxidize quickly and should be put under cold water once cut and drained just before using.

BUTIFARRAS

Fresh sausages filled with seasoned pork or beef then poached to be eaten as is or sliced and browned.

CAFETERAS

Stovetop aluminum Moka espresso makers that come in various sizes and are used to make Cuban espresso.

CALABAZA | MOSCHATA SQUASH

Though it can refer to any starchy, orange-fleshed squash, Cuban recipes call for large West Indian Pumpkins. Sold in chunks at Latin American markets, look for squash with deep orange flesh and no soft spots. Hubbard, butternut, or kabocha squash can also be substituted.

CASQUITOS DE GUAYABA | GUAVA SHELLS

Peeled guava shells poached in syrup are often served with fresh farmer cheese or cream cheese and crackers as a snack or dessert.

CHAYOTE

A pale green fruit with white, mild-flavored flesh that can be cooked or eaten raw in salads.

CHORIZO

Spanish pork sausage seasoned with paprika and used both cured and semi-cured. It can be lightly sautéed in oil to extract its color or eaten as is.

CHURRERA

A metal or plastic tube that is filled with churro batter and squeezed from one end to extract the dough.

COMINO | CUMIN

A pungent and woody spice that is often used in sofritos and marinades. Whole cumin seeds have a longer shelf life and can be ground as needed for maximum freshness.

CULANTRO

This pungent herb with long serrated leaves is a cousin of cilantro but with much stronger flavor. Also known as *recao*, it can be substituted with cilantro.

ENCHILADOS
Shellfish cooked in a tomato-based sauce with a hint of heat from either fresh peppers or pepper-based sauces such as Tabasco sauce.

ESPUMERA
This flat wire-mesh strainer is used to skim impurities that float on the surface of a simmering broth.

ESPUMITA
The frothy light-brown *crema* that forms along the top of Cuban espresso is made by vigorously beating the first few drops of coffee extracted from the moka pot with sugar to form a light-colored paste. The rest of the coffee is then poured over the beaten sugar.

FALDA | FLANK STEAK
Simmered with aromatics, this inexpensive cut of beef was often used to make stock. The muscle fibers break down as it cooks and shred easily, making it ideal for *Vaca Frita* and *Ropa Vieja*.

FLANERA
This stainless steel mold used to cook flan is fitted with a pressure-clipped lid that prevents water from touching the custard as it cooks in a water bath.

FRIJOLES | BEANS
This is a generic term for beans, though black beans (*frijoles negros*) and red beans (frijoles colorados) are the two most popular. They should be rinsed and picked through before using and most recipes call for soaking them in cold water 8 hours or overnight. Other popular beans include *alubia*, chickpeas, lentils, and white navy beans.

FRUTA BOMBA | PAPAYA
This large oval-shaped fruit with yellow skin and bright-orange flesh is eaten as is or used in milk shakes, ice cream, and salads.

GALLETAS | CUBAN CRACKERS
These lightly toasted crackers have a buttery, sturdy texture and are often served with fruit preserves and cream cheese as a dessert. Finely ground, they are also a popular breading.

GUANÁBANA | SOURSOP
This green fruit with a white flesh is native to the island and used to make juice, ice creams, and candies.

GUARAPO | SUGARCANE JUICE
Sold at fruit stands, *ventanitas*, and lunch counters, this natural sugarcane juice is extracted by passing sugarcane stalks through a hand-cranked or powered machine.

GUAYABA | GUAVA
Small green fruit with a pinkish red flesh that can be eaten on its own or used in ice cream, jellies, marmalades, preserves, and drinks.

HARINA | CORNMEAL
Finely ground cornmeal cooked with milk or water to make a polenta-like porridge.

HIERBA BUENA | SPEARMINT
A close cousin of peppermint, spearmint is used to make mojitos.

HOJA DE LAUREL | BAY LEAVES
Used in dry form, this leaf is a common ingredient in stocks, soups, and marinades and valued for its woody, floral, and eucalyptus flavors.

JAMÓN DE COCINAR | COOKING HAM
This frequently used smoked cooking ham is used for a variety of soups and stews.

MALANGA
Also called yautía or cocoyam, this large tuber can be either white or yellow. The yellow *malanga* has a tough yellow flesh and must be eaten immediately after cooking. The white *malanga* turns slightly gray when boiled. Both can be boiled, fried, or added to soups.

MAMEY
Tropical fruit with brown skin, velvety orange-to red-colored flesh, and a large black seed in the middle. It can be eaten as is when ripe or made into shakes and ice cream.

MANTECA | LARD
Rendered pork fat used for frying and in sauces like *Mojo Criollo*. The quality found in supermarkets varies wildly and it is worth seeking out freshly rendered lard from butcher shops or specialty stores.

MARIQUITAS
Green plantains that are thinly sliced and deep fried. They are also called chicharritas.

MOJO CRIOLLO
This blend of sour orange juice, garlic, oregano, cumin, and salt can be used fresh or cooked with hot lard or olive oil to make a sauce.

ÑAME | WHITE YAM
Known as tropical or African white yam, this large starchy tuber with white, yellow, or pink flesh has a tough brown skin. Ñame can be boiled, fried, roasted, or smoked.

NARANJA AGRIA | SOUR ORANGE
Also known as Seville oranges, they were brought to Cuba via Spain. If not available, equal parts of freshly squeezed orange and lime juice can be substituted.

OLLA DE PRESIÓN | PRESSURE COOKER
This deep aluminum pot with a lockable lid and a steam valve is capable of rapidly cooking tough cuts of meat and beans in shorter amounts of time due to its ability to raise internal temperatures beyond the boiling point. Use with caution and do not open until it has cooled properly per manufacturer's instructions.

PAN CUBANO | CUBAN BREAD
This pale, baguette-shaped loaf of bread has a soft interior and thin, papery crust. It can be made with lard (*pan de manteca*) or only water (*pan de agua*).

PASTELITOS
Sweet puff pastries filled with guava, cream cheese, coconut, ham, or beef hash. These are enjoyed for breakfast or in miniature sizes at parties.

PIMENTÓN | SPANISH PAPRIKA
A spice made from ground red chili peppers that varies in heat from sweet to mild or hot.

PLANCHA
This metal sandwich press consists of two flat griddles used for pressing Cuban sandwiches.

PLÁTANO BURRO | DONKEY PLANTAIN
These are similar to regular plantains, except for their shorter appearance and softer taste. They make excellent tostones.

PLÁTANO MADURO | RIPE PLANTAIN
A ripe plantain that's mostly black, it's most often fried and served as a side dish.

PLÁTANO PINTÓN
A medium-ripe plantain that is completely yellow and sweet but firm enough to keep its shape when boiled or added to soups or stews.

PLÁTANO VERDE | GREEN PLANTAIN
These unripe green plantains are used for making *mariquitas* and *tostones*. The peel is notoriously difficult to remove, and should be carefully slit down the middle with a sharp knife and peeled away. Once sliced, they should be kept in water with lime juice to prevent discoloration then drained before using.

QUIMBOMBÓ | OKRA
Brought to Cuba from Africa in the sixteenth century, these small, barrel-shaped pods are the base of soups and stews made with combinations of slab bacon, pork, ham, chorizo, chicken, or *tasajo*.

SOFRITO
A trinity of chopped onions, peppers, and garlic that forms the base of many Cuban dishes.

TASAJO | SALT-CURED BEEF
This salt-cured beef must be soaked and rinsed in several changes of cold water to remove the salt before consumption.

TOCINO | SALT-CURED PORK BELLY
This salt-cured pork belly is similar to slab bacon.

TOSTONERA
This small wooden or metal press is hinged together to evenly mash plantains before a second frying. Wooden *tostoneras* for making stuffed tostones are available online and at Latin American grocery stores.

TOSTONES | FRIED GREEN PLANTAINS
Green plantains cut into rounds, fried, and then smashed into a disc with a tostonera before being fried a second time and served hot as a side dish with salt.

VINO SECO | COOKING WINE
Dry cooking wine.

YUCA | CASSAVA OR MANIOC
A starchy root vegetable native to Latin America, yuca has a thick brown skin that must be peeled. The bitter variety is toxic and must be processed before consumption though it is rarely exported. The sweet variety can be found in grocery stores, but must also be cooked before eating. A layer of wax is placed on it to prevent it from drying out.

RESOURCES

Almost all of the ingredients called for in this book are increasingly available in large-chain supermarkets with well-stocked international food sections. There are also many specialized, online sources offering high-quality ingredients both from Latin America and Spain that go a long way toward building a traditional Cuban pantry. Here are a few worth exploring.

AMIGO FOODS
Online grocery store specializing in Latin American imports and Cuban staples.
www.amigofoods.com
(800) 627-2544

BOB'S RED MILL
Employee-owned company with extensive line of organic whole grains, beans, cornmeal, and fresh milled flours.
www.bobsredmill.com
(800) 349-2173

CUBAN FOOD MARKET
Wide array of Cuban cookware, specialty-food items, and staple pantry ingredients.
www.cubanfoodmarket.com
(877) 999-9945

DESPAÑA BRAND FOODS
Purveyor's of high-quality Spanish cured meats, grains, oils, vinegars, and seasonings.
www.despanabrandfoods.com
(212) 219-5050

FLORIDA CRYSTALS
Wonderful line of organic granulated sugar and demerara sugar available in health food stores.
www.floridacrystals.com
(877) 835-2828

IMUSA
Hispanic cookware, appliances, and gadgets including calderos, morteros, and tostoneras.
www.imusausa.com
(800) 850-2501

LA TIENDA
Online resource for traditional Spanish ingredients.
www.latienda.com
(800) 710-4304

MELISSA'S PRODUCE
Incredible selection of seasonally available tropical fruits and vegetables.
www.melissas.com
(800) 588-0151

OLATZ
Lovely line of Havana inspired table linens based in New York.
www.olatz.com
(212) 255-8627

PENZEY'S SPICES
Eclectic selection of international spices, herbs, and seasonings.
www.penzeys.com
(800) 741-7787

RANCHO GORDO
California-based company specializing in new world heirloom beans, grains, herbs, and spices.
www.ranchogordo.com
(707) 259-1935

ACKNOWLEDGMENTS

There hasn't been a single day I've worked on this book that I haven't been reminded of the generosity of colleagues, friends, and family who gave so much of themselves to help make it happen. Pulling together a list of names is a daunting task, so I'll start at the beginning.

I'd like to thank my friend Isabel González-Whitaker, who always makes sure I am at the right place at the right time. To Ellen Silverman, I couldn't have imagined how far this book would take us, but I'm grateful to have such an incredible wealth of images and experiences to show for it. I'd like to thank Harriet Bell for walking me through the proposal stage with patience and humor and introducing us to our wonderful agent Meg Thompson, who saw us through to the end. I'm also grateful to Matthew Shear who helped us find a home at St. Martin's Press. Once there, I couldn't imagine better collaborators than our editor BJ Berti, Michelle McMillian, Courtney Littler, and Jane Liddle. BJ, your open embrace for what this book could become has meant the world.

I was so happy Jan Derevjanik joined us and seeing all of our work come together in her lovely design has been thrilling. I need to thank our prop stylist Lucy Attwater and food stylist Rebecca Jurkevich for the care they took getting everything exactly right. Lastly, I'd like to thank my research assistant Miguel Massens for his unflagging enthusiasm and dedication.

As a first-time author, I was lucky to have a network of writers, cooks, and chefs who'd been there before and were willing to share their insights and guidance. For this, I'd like to thank: Achy Obejas, Natalie Bovis, Dawn Casale, Lourdes Castro, Betty Cortina-Weiss, David Crofton, Kathy De Witt See, Lydia Martin, Mirta Ojito, Elizabeth Peréz, Luis Pous, Douglas Rodríguez, Leticia Moreinos Schwartz, and Annette Tomei. I came to this field relatively late and will always feel indebted to Melissa Clark, Maricel Presilla, and Judiaann Woo for their early encouragement. I'd especially like to thank Steven Shaw for his beyond the call mentorship and support. I don't know if he realized what he was signing up for when I signed up for his class, but I will be forever grateful that I did.

This book wouldn't have been possible without friends who came through in countless and unexpected ways. For this, I'd like to thank: Magaly Acosta and Orestes Quiñones, Danis Montero Ascanio, the Budet family, Aaron Cedolia, Esther María Fontova, Pat de la Rosa, Luis García and family, Teresa and Luis Gispert, Felice and Bianca Gorordo, Giovanny Gutierrez, Tony Jiménez, Bruce Loshusan, Kat Lee, Nathalie Marcos, Julia and Alfredo Miel, Natalia Martínez, the Marzo family, Craig Shillito, Nicole Valls, Mario Vergel, and everyone at el cortadito and the Cuban Heritage Collections. I'd especially like to thank Humberto and Carmen Calzada who opened so many doors for me.

Living in Brooklyn, my resources went far beyond what my small test kitchen could manage. I'd like to thank the people at G. Esposito & Sons, Fish Tales, Los Paisanos, Staubitz Market, and Union Market for answering every question without making me feel like I was holding up the line.

The Lizama family is large, but their willingness to be part of every project, idea, or notion I can come up with, makes it feel very small—please accept my heartfelt *acaracachin*. I'd also like to thank Alicia Figueredo and Georgina Ponzoa for taking such good care of the Peláez family recipes for anyone who might need them.

I'd like to thank my father for leaving me with an insatiable curiosity about food and the stories that could come from it. I would have so loved to have shared this experience with you. I don't know that I could ever adequately thank my mother Ali, whose absolute belief in me has made me fearless when it really mattered. To my sister Carmen, you not only stayed by my side through every challenge, but somehow made me laugh through it as well.

Finally, I'd like to offer my deepest thanks to each and every one of the contributors who shared their recipes. I'll always be grateful for the time you gave me in your kitchens and around your tables. I'm so happy to share this book with you.

—A.S.P.

The Cuban Table *would not have been possible without the help and encouragement of so many people. To all of them I extend my heartfelt thanks:*

To my husband, Josh, and our son, Luca, for always encouraging me to follow my dreams and supporting me while I worked on the book, which included enduring my many absences while I traveled to Cuba and Miami.

To Ana Sofía Peláez, my partner in *The Cuban Table*, who put her heart and soul into meticulously collecting the recipes and stories that make Cuban food come alive in this book. Her passion for her culture and its food is evident throughout.

To Reid Callanan, of the Santa Fe Photographic Workshop, who first invited me to Cuba.

To Harriet Bell for encouraging me to pursue this project, and for introducing me to Ana and to Meg Thompson, our literary agent extraordinaire.

To the team at St. Martin's Press: Publisher Matthew Shear, who embraced this project from the moment we first discussed it, and who is dearly missed; BJ Berti, who enthusiastically shepherded this book from the beginning and has been a precise, clear and patient editor and guide; Michelle McMillian, whose keen eye and talent as art director is evident throughout; and to the most organized editorial assistant, Courtney Littler. To Jan Derevjanik, who carefully listened to a long list of design wishes and, as if by magic, designed this stunning book.

To prop stylist Lucy Attwater, who brought her sophisticated, refined eye and love of texture and context to the photographs.

To Rebecca Jurkevich, Cuban-American food stylist, whose styling lends an air of grace, beauty, and authenticity to each plate of food.

To Ali Peláez and Carmen Peláez, Ana's mother and sister, who acted as the support team in Miami.

To all of the home cooks and chefs in New York, Miami, and Cuba who graciously and, in some cases, spontaneously opened their kitchens to share their family recipes and stories. Without them, *The Cuban Table* would not have been possible.

A special thank-you to Cuban artist Humberto Calzado and his wife, Carmen, who hosted a Cuban-style family meal in their beautiful garden in Miami. To Nereida and Antonio Pardo, who spent the morning shopping and preparing *frituras* while I photographed them. And to everyone else, both on and off the island, who helped along the way, I want to extend my grateful thanks for your generosity, openness, and support.

Lastly, an enormous thank-you to my Cuban connection, Carlos Otero Blanco, who tirelessly and cheerfully drove me from one end of Cuba to the other as I took the photographs for this book. Carlos shared rum, stories, and introduced me to his favorite *paladares*, where we ate indescribably delicious meals of slow-cooked pork, spicy lamb, and far too much flan.

—*E.S.*

INDEX

A

a caballo, 308
Academia Provincial de Artes
  Plásticas, Santiago, 178
achiote (annatto), 308
  oil, 298
Acosta, Magaly, 27
Aguacate Relleno (Stuffed
  Avocado), 214
ají (bell pepper), 308
Ajiaco Criollo con Casabe (Creole
  Stew with Yuca Flatbread),
  104, 105–7
ají cachucha (pepper), 308
ají guaguao (pepper), 308
alcaparras (capers), 121, 308
Alfonso y Rodríguez, Dolores,
  243
Alicia (grandmother), 157
almíbar (simple sugar syrup), 308
Áloma, Dora, 242
Álvarez, Danielle, 174
Anise Fritters with Syrup
  (Buñuelos de Anis con
  Almíbar), 250, 251
annón (custard apple), 308
arroz (rice), 308. See also rice
  Blanco, 121, 158
  con Garbanzos, 120
  con Leche, 242
  Minutas con Arroz a lo
    Surgidero de Batabanó and,
    200, 201–2
  Negro con Calamares, 132
  con Pollo a la Chorrera, 128–29
  con Pollo, 111, 126, 127
Ávila Alfonso, Dayron, 164
Avocado Salad (Ensalada de
  Aguacate), 211
azafrán (saffron), 308
¡Azucar! Ice Cream Company,
  Little Havana, 270, 272–73,
  273

B

bacalao (salt cod), 309
  Frituras de, 203
Bacardi Massó, Don Facundo, 287
Baked Chocolate Ice Cream "El
  Carmelo," 278–80, 279
Baked Eggs in Rolls (Huevos en
  Acemitas), 137
bakery items, 20–21, 29,
  30–31. See also croquettes;
  marmalades; pastelitos;
  sweets/desserts
  Chiviricos, 34, 35
  Coffee, Cuban, 44, 45–47, 46
  Croquettes, 35, 36–39, 39
  Empanadas, Chorizo, 32–33, 35,
    43, 262
  Guava Layered Cake, 5, 22
  Marmalades, 19, 26, 27–29
  Pastries, Assorted, 15–16, 17–18,
    19, 262
  Poundcakes, Miniature, 13,
    23–25, 24
  Stuffed Potatoes, 42–44
baño maría (water baths), 247–48,
  309
Barrio (barman), 289
Batidos (Tropical Fruit Shakes),
  56, 76, 77
Battle, Suzy, 270, 273
bean(s) (frijoles), 110, 117
  pottage, 113–20, 115, 118
  and Rice, Eastern-Style, 111,
    124, 125
  rinsing of, 310
beef
  Braised, with Peppers and
    Onions, 32, 162–63, 163, 310
  fritas, 51, 62, 63–64, 64, 121, 158,
    159, 310
  Lime-Marinated Crispy, 121,
    158, 159, 310
  Picadillo, Classic, 43, 156, 157,
    222, 223

Pot Roast, Stuffed, 154
  Steak, Pan-Fried, 141, 152–53
  Stew, with Fingerling Potatoes
    and Baby Heirloom Carrots,
    160, 161
  Stock, 306
Benítez Otero, Sofia, 169
Bermúdez, Apolonia "Poli," 212
bijol (condiment), 309
Bistec de Palomilla (Pan-Fried
  Steak), 141, 152–53
Bistec Empanizado (Chicken-Fried
  Steak), 152–53
Black Bean Pottage (Potaje de
  Frijoles Negros), 1, 113–14,
  115
Black-Eyed Pea Fritters (Bollitos
  de Carita), 68, 72, 73
Black Rice with Squid (Arroz
  Negro con Calamares), 132
Boliche Mechado (Stuffed Pot
  Roast), 154
Bollitos de Carita (Black-Eyed Pea
  Fritters), 68, 72, 73
boniato (batata/camote), 2, 89, 90,
  209, 309
The Book of Jewish Food (Roden),
  8
Bouteiller, José León, 287
Braised Beef with Peppers and
  Onions (Ropa Vieja, "Old
  Clothes"), 32, 162–63, 163,
  310
Bread + Butter, Coral Gables, 38,
  40–41
Breaded Fish Sandwich (Pan con
  Minuta), 68–70, 71
Budet, María, 237
Bufill, Olga, 248
Buñuelos de Anis con Almíbar
  (Anise Fritters with Syrup),
  250, 251
Butifarras (Fresh Pork Sausages),
  4, 40, 174–75, 175, 309

C

Cabrera, Alberto, 38, *40–41*

Café con Leche (coffee drink), 45

Café Cubano (Cuban Coffee), *44*, 45–47, *46*

cafeteras (espresso makers), 309

Cake Cubano (Cuban Layer Cake), 258–59

calabaza (moschata squash), 209, 309

  Flan de, 249

  Fritters, 228, *229*

  with Mojo, 224–25

Caldo Gallego (Galician Stew), 81, 102–3

Calzada, Carmen, 126

Calzada, Margot, 204

La Camaronera, Little Havana, 68, *69*, 70, *71*, 73

Camarones Enchilados (Creole Shrimp), 32, 136, 183, *188*, 189, 310

Capuchino Cake, 244–45, *245*

El Carmelo, Havana, 278

Carne con Papas y Zanahorias (Beef Stew with Fingerling Potatoes and Baby Heirloom Carrots), *160*, 161

Carne de Cerdo Adobado (Pork Loin in Adobo), 178–79

Casabe (Yuca Flatbread), *104*, 105–7

Casquitos de Guayaba (Poached Guava Shells), 157, 262, 266, *267*, 309

Castro, Lourdes, 158

Changó (deity), 96

Le Chansonnier, Havana, 164

chayote fruit, 209, 309

Cherimoya Ice Cream (Helado de Cherimoya), 275

Chez Panisse restaurant, 174

Chicharritas (Plantain Chips), 74, *75*, 86, *86*

Chicharrones de Puerco (Pork Belly Rinds), 2, 215, *216*, 217, 225

chicken

  Creole Fried, *148*, 149

  Croquettes, 37

Fricasée, 22, 121, 141, 150–51

  -Fried Steak, 152–53

  Noodle Soup, 87

  Pie, 143–44, (145–46), 147

  with Rice, 111, 126, *127*, 128–29

  Stock, 306–7

Chickpea Stew (Potaje de Garbanzos), *118*, 119–20

Chilindrón de Chivo (Goat Stew), 164–65

Chiviricos, 34, *35*

Chocolate Rum Ice Cream, 278, 280

chorizo (sausage), 309

  Empanadas, 32–33, *35*, 43, 262

  Tortilla de Papas y, 133

Chorote con Churros (Hot Chocolate Churros), 281–83, *282–83*

La Chorrera del Vedado, Havana, 128

Christie, Anna, 242

Classic Beef Picadillo (Picadillo Clásico), 43, *156*, 157, *222*, 223

Cocina Criolla (Villapol), 42

La Cocina de Lilliam, Miramar, 89, *100–101*, 101

cocktails

  Crema de Vie, 295

  Cuba Libre, 289

  Daiquirí, 294

  Mojito, 290, *291*

  El Presidente, 289

coconut, *263*

  and Almond Candy Cones, 4, *264*, 265

  Cookies, Crispy, 265

  Cornmeal Cake with Guava and, 256, *257*

  Ice Cream, 253, 275–76

  milk, 298

  Sauce, 194, *195*

  Sweetened, 19, 22, *260*, 262, 266

Coco Quemado (Crispy Coconut Cookies), 265

Cod Fish Fritters (Frituras de Bacalao), 203

Coffee, Cuban (Café Cubano), *44*, 45, *46*, 47

colada, 13

comino (cumin), 309

Congrí Oriental (Eastern-Style Red Beans and Rice), 111, *124*, 125

corn, 209

  husking/steaming of, 212–13

Cornmeal Cake with Coconut and Guava (Pan de Maíz con Coco y Guayaba), 256, *257*

Cornmeal Stew with Crab (Harina con Cangrejo), 190, *191*

Corn Tamale (Tamal de Maíz), 212–13, *213*

Coro, Margot, 244

Cortado (coffee drink), 45

Cox, Jennings, 294

Crema de Boniato, 89, 90

Crema de Malanga (Cream of Malanga Soup), 81, 83

Crema de Vie (Cuban Egg Nog), 295

Creole flavors, 1, 5

Creole Fried Chicken (Pollo Frito a la Criolla), *148*, 149

Creole Garlic Sauce (Mojo Criollo), 169, 301, 311

Creole Shrimp (Camarones Enchilados), 32, 136, 183, *188*, 189, 310

Creole Stew with Yuca Flatbread (Ajiaco Criollo con Casabe), *104*, 105–7

croquettes (croquetas)

  Chicken, 37

  Ham, *35*, 36–37, 53, 55

  Midnight, 38–39, *39*

  Preparada, 53, 55

  Spinach, 37

Cruz, Celia, 273

Cruz, José María, 25

Cruz, Pilar, 25

Cruz, Roger, 25

Cuba, 1–3, *3–4*, *6–7*, *9*, *78–80*, *91*, *110*, *123*, *136*, *138–40*, *144*, *151*, *153*, *155*, *176–77*, *182*, *211*, *220–21*, *226–27*, *249*, *277*, *284–86*

  food evolution in, 4–5, 8

  regional fare in, 194

sandwich counters in, 51
  War of Independence in, 289
Cuba Libre (Rum and Coke), 289
Cuban Layer Cake (Cake
  Cubano), 258–59
Cuban Sandwich, 53–55, 58–59,
  178
Cuban-Style Hamburgers with
  Shoestring Fries (Fritas al
  Caballo con Papitas a la
  Juliana), 62, 63–64, 64
Cucuruchos de Coco y Almendras
  (Coconut and Almond Candy
  Cones), 4, 264, 265
culantro/recao (herb), 309

D

Daiquirí, 294
Daiquirí Frappé, 294
de la Torre, Isabel, 273
del Corral, Eloina, 293
del Corral, Victor, 293
Delicias de la Mesa--Manual de
  Cocina y Repostería (Reyes
  Gavilán y Moenck), 304
Deus (bartender), 290
Díaz-Bergnes, Clarita, 201
Díaz Moreno, Ana, 196
Domínguez Palenzuela, Cleo, 101
Domínguez Palenzuela, Lilliam,
  89, 100, 101
Drake, Sir Francis, 290
Drenched Chicken and Rice
  (Arroz con Pollo a la
  Chorrera), 128–29
Dulce de Coco (Sweetened
  Coconut), 19, 22, 260, 262,
  266
Dulce de Tomate (Tomato Jam),
  260, 261

E

Eastern-Style Red Beans and Rice
  (Congrí Oriental), 111, 124,
  125
Egg Custard (Natilla), 240, 241
eggs (huevos), 109–10, 131,
  136–37
Elena Ruz Sandwich, 65
Empanaditas de Chorizo (Chorizo

Empanada), 32–33, 35, 262
Empanaditas, Picadillo, 43
enchilados, 32, 136, 183, 188, 189,
  310
Ensalada de Aguacate (Avocado
  Salad), 211
Escabeche (Pickled Fish), 183,
  204–5, 205
Esperanza (Cuban cook), 281
espumera (strainer), 310
espumita (froth), 310
La Estrella Chocolate Factory,
  Havana, 22

F

falda (flank steak), 310
Fiery Oxtail (Rabo Encendido),
  168
Figueredo, Alicia, 258
Fish and Leek Soup (Pescado en
  Salsa de Perro Caibarién),
  94, 95
Fish in Coconut Sauce (Pescado en
  Salsa de Coco), 194, 195
flan de Calabaza, 249
flan de Coco, 248
flan de Leche, 1, 246, 247
flan de Queso, 249
flanera (steel mold), 310
foundation recipes
  Achiote Oil, 298
  Coconut Milk, 298
  Creole Garlic Sauce, 169, 301,
    311
  Pan de Agua, 53, 299, 311
  Pan de Manteca, 2, 299, 311
  Pan de Media Noche, 57, 300
  Sofrito, 305, 312
  Stock, Beef, 306
  Stock, Chicken, 306–7
  Stock, Fish, 307
  Tomato Purée (Puré de
    Tomate), 96, 304
French Laundry restaurant, 174
Fresh Pork Sausages (Butifarras),
  4, 40, 174–75, 175, 309
Fricasé de Pollo (Chicken
  Fricasée), 22, 121, 141, 150–51
Fried Fish with Plantain
  Chips (Pescado Frito con

Mariquitas), 196–97, 199
Fried Plantain Chips with
  Lime-Cilantro Vinaigrette
  (Mariquitas con Vinagreta de
  Cilantro y Limón), 74, 75
Fried Pork Chunks (Masas de
  Puerco), 4, 4, 172, 173
Fried Ripe Plantain Omelet
  (Tortilla de Plátanos
  Maduros), 134, 135
Frijoles Dormidos, 114
Fritas al Caballo con Papitas
  a la Juliana (Cuban-Style
  Hamburgers with Shoestring
  Fries), 62, 63–64, 64
Frituras de Bacalao (Cod Fish
  Fritters), 203
Frituras de Calabaza (Calabaza
  Fritters), 228, 229
Frituras de Malanga (Malanga
  Latkes), 230, 231
fruit(s), 92, 207–8, 219, 220–21,
  225–27, 262–63, 274. See also
  vegetables
  Avocado Salad, 211
  Avocado, Stuffed, 214
  Calabaza Fritters, 228, 229
  Calabaza with Mojo, 224–25
  Malanga Latkes and, 230, 231
  Plantains, Mashed, with Pork
    Rinds, 215, 216, 217
  Plantains, Simmered, with Lime
    Vinaigrette, 218
  shakes, tropical, 56, 76, 77
  Tostones, Stuffed with Beef
    Picadillo, 43, 222, 223
fruta bomba (papaya), 209, 310
Fufú de Plátano con Chicharrones
  de Puerco (Mashed Plantain
  with Pork Rinds), 215, 216,
  217

G

Galician Stew (Caldo Gallego),
  81, 102–3
galletas (Cuban crackers), 310
Garbanzos
  Fritos, 120
  with rice, 120
  Stew, 118, 119–20

García, Arsenio, 70
García, David, 70
García, Esteban, 70, 193
García, Esteban, Jr., 193
García, Felix, 70
García, Juan, 70
García, Luis, 193
García, Maria Luisa, 185, 193
García, Mario, 70
García, Maritza, 70, 73
García, Ramón, 70
Garcia's Seafood, Miami, *192–93*, 193
Garlic Soup with Poached Eggs (Sopa de Ajo con Huevos), 84, *85*
Gispert, Luis, 77
Goat Stew (Chilindrón de Chivo), 164–65
Gómez Betancourt, Encarnación, 143, *146–47*, 147
Gómez Betancourt, Mario, 147
Gómez de Dumois, Ana Dolores, 243
González, Mercedes, 63
González, Victoriano Benito, 63
Greenspan, Mark, 42
guanábana (soursop), 77, 209, 310
guarapo (sugarcane juice), 51, 310
guayaba(s) (guava), 209, 310
    Marmalade, *26*, 27, 266
    Preserves, 27
    Stuffed, 266

H

harina (cornmeal), 310
Harina con Cangrejo (Cornmeal Stew with Crab), 190, *191*
Helado de Cherimoya (Cherimoya Ice Cream), 275
Helado de Coco (Coconut Ice Cream), 253, 275–76
Helado de Fresa (Strawberry Ice Cream), 275, 276
Helado de Mamey Colorado (Red Mamey Ice Cream), 275, 277
Hemingway, Ernest, 290, 294
hierba buena (spearmint), 310
hoja de laurel (bay leaves), 310
Hot Chocolate Churros (Chorote con Churros), 281–83, *282–83*

Huevos a la Malagueña (Málaga-Style Eggs), 136
Huevos en Acemitas (Baked Eggs in Rolls), 137
Hungry Sofia (blog), 2

I

Ice Cream, *271–72*, 273
    Chocolate, Baked "El Carmelo," 278–80, *279*
    Chocolate Rum, 278, 280
    Fruit, 253, 275–77
    Vanilla, Cuban, 270

J

jamón de cocinar (cooking ham), 310
Jiménez, Alicia Navia, 22
Jimenez, Maria, 265
Joffre González, Sara, 96

L

Layered Coffee (El Pecado), *46*, 47
Lechón Asado (Oven-Roasted Pork Shoulder), 60, 141, 169, *171*
Leila's Restaurant, Miami, 152
Lentil Soup with Ripe Plantains (Sopa de Lentejas con Plátanos Maduros), *92*, 93
Lime-Cilantro Vinaigrette, 74, *75*, 203
Lime-Marinated Crispy Beef (Vaca Frita), 121, 158, *159*, 310
Lizama, Marta Fontanills, 137
López Gómez, Carmen, 154
lunches. *See also* sandwich(es)
    Fritters, Black-Eyed Pea, 68, *72*, 73
    Fruit Shakes, Tropical, *56*, *76*, 77
    Plantain Chips with Lime-Cilantro Vinaigrette, 74, *75*
    sandwiches for, *50*, 53–70, *54*, *58–59*, *60–62*, *64*, *71*
lunch/sandwich counters, *48–50*, 51, *54–56*, *60*, *66–67*, *69–71*, *214*
    in Cuba, 51
Lusky, Becky Epelbaum, 218
Lusky, Janice, 42

M

Machado, Gerardo, 289
Málaga-Style Eggs (Huevos a la Malagueña), 136
malanga (yautía/cocoyam), 2, 5, 81, 209, 310
    Latkes, *230*, 231
    Soup, Cream of, 81, 83
mamey (fruit), *274*, 311
    Ice Cream, 275, 277
    Shake, 77
mango, 209
    Marmalade, *26*, 28
    Shake, 77
manteca (lard), 311
Mantecado (Cuban Vanilla Ice Cream), 270
Marcos, Nathalie, 132
Marcos, Olga, 228
El Marino paladar, Cuba, 196
mariquitas/chicharritas (green plantains), 86, 311
Mariquitas con Vinagreta de Cilantro y Limón (Plantain Chips with Lime-Cilantro Vinaigrette), 74, *75*
Mariscos con Salsa de Coco (Shellfish in Coconut Sauce), 194
marmalades, 19
    Guava, *26*, 27, 266
    Mango, *26*, 28
    Papaya, *26*, 29
Martínez, Rafael, 309
Martínez Ybor, Vicente, 55
Masa Real con Guayaba (Guava Layered Cake), 5, 22
Masas de Puerco (Fried Pork Chunks), 4, *4*, 172, *173*
Mashed Plantain with Pork Rinds (Fufú de Plátano con Chicharrones de Puerco), 215, *216*, 217
Massens, Miguel, 105
Matajíbaro, 215
Media Noche (Midnight Sandwich), 55, 57
    Pan de, 57, 300
Medio Dias (Midday Sandwiches), 57

Merenguitos Dormidos (Sleeping Meringues), 237, *238–39*

Meringue Topping, 245

Mermelada de Fruta Bomba (Papaya Marmalade), *26*, 29

Mermelada de Guayaba (Guava Marmalade), *26, 27*, 266

Mermelada de Mango (Mango Marmalade), *26*, 28

Midnight Croquettes (Croquetas de Media Noche), 38–39, *39*

Minutas con Arroz a lo Surgidero de Batabanó (Snapper and Saffron Rice), *200*, 201–2

Miramar Yacht Club, Havana, 290

Mojito, 290, *291*

Mojo Criollo (Creole Garlic Sauce), 169, 301, 311

Molina de Venet, Lucila, 102

Molina de Venet, Siomara, 102

Moros y Cristianos, 114, 169

N

ñame (white yam), 5, 81, 311

naranja agria (sour orange), 311

Natilla (Egg Custard), 240, *241*

Nena (Cuban cook), 1

Nuevo Manual del Cocinero Cubano y Español, 162

O

Okra Stew with Plantain Dumplings (Quimbombó con Bolitas de Plátano), 81, 96–97, *98–99*

olla de presión (pressure cooker), 311

Ortiz, Fernando, 81

Oshún (goddess), 190

Otero Blanco, Carlos, 8

Oven-Roasted Pork Shoulder (Lechón Asado), 60, 141, 169, *171*

ox, *168*

  Fiery, 168

  -tail in Caper Sauce, 121, 166–68, *167*

Oyarzun, Cristina, 128

Oyarzun, Natasha, 150

P

Palacios, Geraldo Alexander, 178

paladares (family-run restaurants), 3, 9

Palomo Camafreita, Aida, 174

Pan con Bistec, 153

Pan con Lechón (Roast Pork Sandwich), 60, *61*

Pan con Minuta (Breaded Fish Sandwich), 68–70, *71*

Pan Cubano (Cuban bread), 311

Pan de Agua, 53, 299, 311

Pan de Maíz con Coco y Guayaba (Cornmeal Cake with Coconut and Guava), 256, *257*

Pan de Manteca, 2, 299, 311

Pan de Media Noche, 57, 300

Paneca, Claudia, 261

Pan-Fried Steak (Bistec de Palomilla), 141, 152–53

Panquecitos (Miniature Poundcakes), 13, 23–25, *24*

Panque de Jamaica, Miami, 13, *24–25*, 25

pantry terms, 308–12

Papas Fritas a la Juliana (Shoestring Fries), *62*, 63–64, *64*, 152

Papas Rellenas (Stuffed Potatoes), 42–44

Pardo, Nereida, 116, 256

Pargo Relleno (Stuffed Snapper), 185, *186–87*

Pastel de Pollo (Chicken Pie), 143–44, (145–46), 147

pastelitos (pastries), 262, 311

  de Guayaba, 16, *17*

  de Queso (cheese), 15, *17*

  de Queso y Guayaba (Cheese and Guayaba), 15, *17*, 19

El Pecado (Layered Coffee), *46*, 47

Peláez del Casal, Amelia, 1

Peláez del Casal, Carmen, 1

Peláez del Casal, Julian, 1, 113

Peláez del Casal, Ninita, 1

Período Especial (Cuban economic crisis), 3

Pescado en Salsa de Coco (Fish in Coconut Sauce), 194, *195*

Pescado en Salsa de Perro Caibarién (Fish and Leek Soup), 94, *95*

Pescado Frito con Mariquitas (Fried Fish with Plantain Chips), 196–97, *199*

Petit, Alfred, 128

Picadillo al Caballo, 157

Picadillo Clásico (Classic Beef Picadillo), 43, *156*, 157, *222*, 223

Pickled Fish (Escabeche), 183, 204–5, *205*

pimentón (Spanish paprika), 311

plancha (sandwich press), 55, 311

plantain(s) (plátano), 209

  chips, 74, *75*, 86, *86*, 196–97, *199*

  donkey (burro), 311

  dumplings, 81, 96–97, *98–99*

  fried green, 86, 311

  green (verde), 311

  mashed, with pork rinds, 215, *216*, 217

  medium-ripe (pintón), 311

  omelet, *134*, 135

  ripe (maduro), *92*, 93, 157, 158, 311

  simmered, with lime vinaigrette, 218

  soups, 86, *92*, 93

  tart, *252*, 253

Plátanos Sancochados con Vinagreta de Limón (Simmered Plantains with Lime Vinaigrette), 218

Poached Guava Shells (Casquitos de Guayaba), 157, 262, 266, *267*, 309

Pollo Frito a la Criolla (Creole Fried Chicken), *148*, 149

pork

  Chunks, Fried, 4, *4*, 172, *173*

  Croquettes, 35, 36–39, *39*, 53, 55

  Loin, in Adobo, 178–79

  Sausages, Fresh, 4, 40, 174–75, *175*, 309

  Shoulder, Oven-Roasted, 60, 141, 169, *171*

Pork Belly Rinds (Chicharrones de Puerco), 2, 215, *216*, 217, 225

Potaje de Frijoles Colorados (Red Bean Pottage), 111, 116
Potaje de Frijoles Negros (Black Bean Pottage), 1, 113–14, *115*
Potaje de Garbanzos (Chickpea Stew), *118*, 119–20
pottage (potaje), 1, 111–20, *115*, *118*
El Presidente, 289
Principe de Gales (cigars), 55
Pujals, Victor, 53

Q

quimbombó (okra), 312
  con Bolitas de Plátano, 81, 96–97, *98–99*

R

Rabo Alcaparrado (Oxtail in Caper Sauce), 121, 166–68, *167*
Rabo Encendido (Fiery Oxtail), 168
Ramóm (grandfather), 133
Red Bean Pottage (Potaje de Frijoles Colorados), 111, 116
Red Beans and Rice, Eastern-Style (Congrí Oriental), 111, *124*, 125
resources, cooking, 313
El Rey de las Fritas, Little Havana, 63
Reyes Gavilán y Moenck, María Antonieta, 304
Ribalaigua Vert, Constantino "Constante," 294
rice (arroz), *110. See also* arroz
  Black, with Squid, 132
  Chicken and, 111, 126, *127*
  Drenched Chicken and, 128–29
  Garbanzos and, 120
  Pudding, 242
  Red Beans and, 111, *124*, 125
  rinsing tips for, 121
  Snapper and Saffron, *200*, 201–2
  White, 121, 158
Rivera, Jennifer, 231
Rivera, Mariana, 231
Rivera, Pepito, 231
Roast Pork Sandwich (Pan con

Lechón), 60, *61*
Roden, Claudia, 8
Rodríguez-Duarte, Rosa, 250
Rodríguez, Dulce, 122, *122*
Rodríguez, Gertrudis, 122, *122*, 266
Rodríguez, Nena, 119, 122
Ropa Vieja "Old Clothes" (Braised Beef with Peppers and Onions), 32, 162–63, *163*, 310
Rum, Cuban, 287. *See also* cocktails

S

Sabater, Cristina, 34
Sabater, Rosa, 125
Salsa Picante, 196–97, *197*
sandwich(es), *54, 60*
  Cuban, 53–55, *58–59*, 178
  Elena Ruz, 65
  Fish, Breaded, 68–70, *71*
  fritas, 51, *62, 63–64, 64*, 121, 158, *159*, 310
  Hamburgers with Shoestring Fries, Cuban-Styled, *62, 63–64, 64*
  Midday, 57
  Midnight, 55, 57, 300
  Pork Roast, 60, *61*
Santamarina, Carlos, 47
Santeiro, Nena, 289
Santi's restaurant, Cuba, 183
seafood, *182*
  in Coconut Sauce, 194, *195*
  Crab and Cornmeal Stew, 190, *191*
  Fried, with Plantain Chips, 196–97, *199*
  Frituras de Bacalao, 203
  Pickled, 183, 204–5, *205*
  prevalence, in Cuba, of, 183
  Sandwich, Breaded, 68–70, *71*
  Shrimp, Creole, 32, 136, 183, *188*, 189, 310
  Snapper and Saffron Rice, *200*, 201–2
  Snapper, Stuffed, 185, *186–87*
  Soup, with Leek, 94, *95*
  Stock, 307

shakes, *56, 76*, 77
Shellfish in Coconut Sauce (Mariscos con Salsa de Coco), 194
Shoestring Fries (Papas Fritas a la Juliana), *62, 63–64, 64*, 152
Siboney people, 5, 81
Simmered Plantains with Lime Vinaigrette (Plátanos Sancochados con Vinagreta de Limón), 218
Sleeping Meringues, (Merenguitos Dormidos), 237, *238–39*
Snapper and Saffron Rice (Minutas con Arroz a lo Surgidero de Batabanó), *200*, 201–2
Sofrito (sauce base), 305, 312
Sopa de Ajo con Huevos, 84, *85*
Sopa de Lentejas con Plátanos Maduros, *92*, 93
Sopa de Plátano, 86
Sopa de Pollo con Fideos, 87
soup (sopa). *See also* stew(s)
  Boniato, Cream of, 89, 90
  Chicken Noodle, 87
  Fish and Leek, 94, *95*
  Garlic with Poached Eggs, 84, *85*
  Lentil, with Ripe Plantains, *92*, 93
  Malanga, Cream of, 81, 83
  Plantain, 86
  Tamal, in pot, *88*, 89
Soursop Shake (Batido de Guanábana), 77
Spanish-Style Tortilla (Tortillas Española), 133
Spinach Croquettes (Croquetas de Espinaca), 37
Statz, Malu, 47
stew(s). *See also* soup
  Beef, with Fingerling Potatoes and Baby Heirloom Carrots, *160*, 161
  Cornmeal and Crab, 190, *191*
  Creole, with Yuca Flatbread, *104*, 105–7
  Galician, 81, 102–3
  Goat, 164–65
  history of Cuban, 83
  Okra with Plantain Dumplings,

81, 96–97, *98–99*
stock, 306–7
Strawberry Ice Cream (Helado de Fresa), 275, 276
Stuffed Avocado (Aguacate Relleno), 214
Stuffed Potatoes (Papas Rellenas), 42–44
Stuffed Pot Roast (Boliche Mechado), 154
Stuffed Snapper (Pargo Relleno), 185, *186–87*
Surtido de Pastelitos (Assorted Pastries), 15–16, *17–18*, 19, 262
Sweetened Coconut (Dulce de Coco), 19, 22, *260*, 262, 266
sweets/desserts, *232–34*, 235, 245, *254–55, 268–69*. *See also* bakery items; Ice Cream
   Anise Fritters with Syrup, 250, *251*
   Capuchino Cake, 244–45, *245*
   Churros, Hot Chocolate, 281–83, *282–83*
   Coconut and Almond Candy Cones, 4, *264*, 265
   Coconut, Sweetened, 19, 22, *260*, 262, 266
   Coco Quemado, 265
   Cornmeal Cake with Coconut and Guava, 256, *257*
   Egg Custard, 240, *241*
   Flan, Calabaza, 249
   Flan, Coconut, 248
   Flan, Cream Cheese, 249
   Flan de Leche, 1, *246*, 247
   Guava Shells, Poached, 157, 262, 266, *267*, 309
   Guavas, Stuffed, 266
   Ice Cream, 270, *271, 274*, 275–80, *279*

Layer Cake, Cuban, 258–59
Meringues, Sleeping, 237, *238–39*
Meringue Topping, 244–45
Plantain Tart, *252*, 253
Rice Pudding, 242
Tomato Jam, *260*, 261
Yemitas, 243

T
Taíno people, 5, 81
Tamal de Maíz (Corn Tamale), 212–13, *213*
Tamal in a Pot (Tamal en Cazuela), *88*, 89
Tampa-Style Sandwich Cubana, 53, 55
Tarte Tentación (Plantain Tart), *252*, 253
tasajo (salt-cured beef), 81, 312
Tembras-Bauza, Rebecca, 166
Tinta y Café, Little Havana, 47
tocino (salt-cured pork belly), 312
Tomato Jam (Dulce de Tomate), *260*, 261
Tomato Purée (Puré de Tomate), 96, 304
Torreón de la Chorrera, Havana, 128
tortilla(s)
   Fried Ripe Plantain Omelet, *134*, 135
   de Papas y Chorizo, 133
   Spanish-Style, 133
tostonera (press), 312
tostones (fried green plantains), 43, 312
   Stuffed with Beef Picadillo, 43, *222*, 223
Tremols, Guillermo, 290
Tropical Fruit Shakes (Batidos), *56, 76*, 77

U
University of Miami's Cuban Heritage Collection, 51

V
Vaca Frita (Lime-Marinated Crispy Beef), 121, 158, *159*, 310
Vale Todo (Brazilian soap opera), 3
vegetables, *206, 208, 220–21, 227*. *See also* fruit(s)
   Avocado Salad, 211
   Avocado, Stuffed, 214
   Corn Tamale, 212–13, *213*
   Malanga Latkes, *230*, 231
   Tostones Stuffed with Beef Picadillo and, 43, *222*, 223
Venet-Jiménez, Lucila, 243
ventanitas (street cafés), *12*, 13, 47
Vergel, Delia, 93
Victor's Cafe, New York City, 161, *292–93*, 293
Villapol, Nitza, 42
vino seco (cooking wine), 312

W
White Rice (Arroz Blanco), 121, 158
Woon, Basil, 294

Y
Yemitas, 243
yuca (cassava/manioc), 209, *225*, 312
   Flatbread, *104*, 105–7
   con Mojo, 169, 225
   Rellena, 44

Z
Zaldívar, Sonia, 161, 293

ANA SOFÍA PELÁEZ grew up in a famous Cuban family as the great-niece of the revered avant-garde painter Amelia Peláez del Casal. Raised in Miami and transplanted to New York, Ana Sofía launched her food blog, Hungry Sofia, in 2008 in an effort to discover the rich smells, heady flavors, and baroque rituals of Latin food. Since then, she has been featured in *The New York Times*, *InStyle* magazine, The Huffington Post, Food 52, Apartment Therapy's the Kitchn, iVillage, and NBC Latino. She's appeared on the Cooking Channel's "Stay Hungry" campaign and Aarón Loves NY with Chef Aarón Sanchez. Most recently, Hungry Sofia was nominated by *Saveur* magazine as one of the Best Regional Cuisine blogs of 2012.